Contents

List of tables and figures v
Acknowledgements vi
Executive summary vii

1 Introduction: challenging images and sustainable regeneration 1
Stigma and sustainable regeneration 1
Marketing, regeneration and the social rented sector 2
Structure of the report 3

2 Different perceptions of three estates 4
Characteristics of focus group participants 4
Attitudes to the estates 4
A typology of attitudes 8
The image of the estates 9
The image of the people 9
The relevance of image 10
What causes the estates' problems? 10
Is the reputation fixed, changing or changeable? 11
Future prospects of the estates 11
Conclusion 13

3 Living with stigma: impacts on life chances 14
Introduction 14
Economic impacts of stigma 14
Stigma and relationships 16
Impacts of stigma on service delivery 19
Experiencing the media 21
The emotional impacts of stigma 21
Conclusion: how stigma is revealed 22

4 Building estate images: key actors and activities 24
Introduction 24
Understanding estate images: a framework 24
Private-sector services and estate images 26
Employers and estate images 29
The media and esate images 29
Conclusion 30

5 The image managers   31
  Introduction   31
  Public services and estate images   31
  Regeneration initiatives and estate images   33
  Managing the media   37
  Conclusion   37

6 Challenging images: suggestions for action   38
  Organising image management   38
  Encouraging the stakeholders   39
  Recruiting the public sector   41
  Managing the media   41
  Targeted image management: residents and potential incomers   42
  Modifying regeneration practice   46
  Conclusion: the need for substantive change   47

7 Challenging images: implications for policy and practice   48
  Implications for regeneration policy   48
  Implications for regeneration practice   48

  References   50
  Appendix A: Research methods   51
  Appendix B: Summary of three estates   52

List of tables and figures

Tables

1	Summary of the responses to positive and negative images of the estates	12
2	Economic impacts of stigma and residents' responses	16
3	Stigma and relationships: impacts and responses	18
4	Service delivery and stigma: impacts and responses	20
5	Building estate images: actors and roles	25
6	Approaches to image management: the case-study initiatives	34
7	The varied impact of messages on target groups	44

Figures

1	Characteristics of focus group participants	4
2	Perceptions of Castle Vale	5
3	Perceptions of Meadow Well	6
4	Perceptions of Pilton	7
5	Warmth towards the estates: a thermometer	9
6	Sensitivity to image management: a thermometer	43

Acknowledgements

We would like to thank all of the people who participated in the research, in particular those individuals who gave up their evenings to attend focus groups. The research would not have been possible without the enthusiastic involvement of the three case-study initiatives, so to the partnerships and their staff, thank you.

We also thank the Joseph Rowntree Foundation, which funded this research within its Area Regeneration Programme. In particular, we thank John Low, the Foundation's Project Manager. The Project Advisory Group offered knowledge advice and guidance throughout the project for which we are indebted. Its members were:

- Ian Cole, School of Urban and Regional Studies, Sheffield Hallam University
- Richard Crossley, PEP North
- Gerard Hastings, Centre for Social Marketing, University of Strathclyde
- Paul Lautman, Local Government Association;
- Jenni Marrow, Pilton Partnership
- Maureen McMillan, Greater Pilton Community Alliance
- Anne Power, CASE, London School of Economics
- Nicholas Schoon, Joseph Rowntree Foundation Journalism Fellow
- Mike Stevenson, Design Links.

Additionally, we would like to acknowledge colleagues at the University of Glasgow for their support and interest. Particular thanks are due to Keith Kintrea for his comprehensive critique of this report in its draft stages and to Julie McKinven for her secretarial assistance.

Executive summary

Many of the UK's worst housing estates do not simply endure material disadvantages, but also suffer from poor reputations. They are viewed as 'problem places', home to 'problem people'. Some have a local infamy for crime or drug abuse, and a few achieve national notoriety. Such a problem reputation can reinforce or even magnify an estate's material difficulties.

This report examines an issue of increasing importance to regeneration initiatives: addressing an area's poor reputation in order to attract and retain tenants, owner-occupiers and business. It is based on the understanding that unless a stigmatised estate can change its local image then regeneration initiatives will not succeed over the longer term. It is likely to be of interest to regeneration initiatives charged with the turnaround of stigmatised estates, but also to landlords and other agencies operating within low demand neighbourhoods.

The report draws on research in three estates in the UK. Each has a significant investment programme underway, each has undergone substantial remodelling as well as addressing economic and social problems, and each continues to have a poor local reputation. They were selected to represent different approaches to the image problem, and because they operate in markedly different housing markets. The research includes: focus groups with over 200 estate residents and non-residents; an exploration of the three regeneration initiatives through interview and documentary analysis; interviews with local employers; and a mystery shopper survey of estate agents.

The research found that in each area a poor reputation is rooted in long-standing beliefs about the estate and its people. There is strong evidence that this translates into a stigma for residents that affects all areas of their lives. They report that they are economically disadvantaged by living on the estate, that their relationships with non-residents are coloured by prejudice, and that they receive lower quality services from both the public and private sector than others in the wider area. In addition, the estate's reputation has an emotional impact felt by virtually all residents, who are angry, hurt and upset by the expressions of stigma that they live with.

The three estates have broadly the same reputation as impoverished housing estates more widely. They are regarded as places of high crime, peopled by the feckless and unemployed. but a key finding is that it is inappropriate to talk of *the image* of an estate. Rather there are *fractured images*. Individuals emphasise different aspects of the estate, and perceive it differently, depending on their own characteristics and experiences. The report identifies six groups on a continuum of warmth towards the estate. These are:

- committed residents
- budding incomers
- potential leavers
- doubtful incomers
- probable leavers
- improbable incomers.

These view the estate, and the estate's residents, in markedly different ways. While committed residents are well connected in the estate's community and see its residents as an asset, the probable leavers and improbable incomers are not connected. These groups have few if any relationships with estate residents and regard its people as threatening and the cause of the area's problems.

Committed residents and budding incomers see image as a very important problem for the estate. They reject the reputation of the area, and blame the media and others for creating and perpetuating stereotypes. The remaining groups, in contrast, believe that reputation and reality coincide. For them it makes no sense to ask what causes the reputation nor how its image can be changed.

Three distinct processes are identified by which a variety of public and private sector actors contribute to images of estates. These are:

- *responding to images:* activities and behaviours which are reactions to an estate's image (conscious or unconscious);
- *shaping images:* activities which inadvertently create or sustain an estate's image, positively or negatively;
- *challenging images:* deliberate actions intended to influence, manage or challenge perceptions of the estate.

The report argues that few actors are involved in challenging images, and that most simply respond to the estate's poor image, or even help to sustain it. A key task, therefore, is to encourage a greater number to play a more positive role. Two strategies for doing this are identified: appealing to the actors' own self-interest by helping them to do their own job more effectively or more profitably; and raising awareness among actors of the damage they may be doing to the estate's sustainability.

In the case-study areas, some attempt has been made to draw private sector agencies into the regeneration process, although only employers have been targeted specifically as part of image management. This contrasts with a lack of attention to the role of public sector agencies who do not tend to be involved specifically in the task of image management, despite their commitment to the wider regeneration process. The research implies that image management cuts across the entire regeneration agenda. An awareness of the 'image effect' should be integral to the full range of activities and programmes undertaken.

The report finds that perceptions of an area lag behind its physical and social change. Unless this is addressed the estates are unlikely to be places of residential choice for households with options and lives of estate residents will continue to be

blighted, so that those who can will continue to leave. Thus, a poor reputation can be a drag on the regeneration process, and must be addressed by initiatives as part of their regeneration strategy.

However, the report concludes that regeneration initiatives can begin to develop a strategic approach to challenging images and a number of suggestions are made on how this could be done. These suggestions cut across the entire regeneration agenda and include developing targeted marketing strategies to attract new residents and to reassure existing residents, encouraging stakeholding among public and private sector actors and developing appropriate organisational arrangements at the estate level. The study also suggests the need to reorientate regeneration activity to increase the profile of the process of change within the wider community. Crucially, the report argues that attempts to challenge images will not be effective unless they are grounded in a changed, or at least changing, reality.

Introduction: challenging images and sustainable regeneration

Can regeneration initiatives help our most disadvantaged housing estates shake off years of stigma and notoriety? This report addresses this critical question for regeneration policy and practice. It draws on the findings from research in three housing estates with poor, or challenging, images, which are also undergoing substantial change as result of a major regeneration initiative. The report provides evidence of the tenacity of stigma on estates, despite significant change. Yet it also argues that problem images can be challenged and provides some practical suggestions for regeneration initiatives in tackling this task.

Stigma and sustainable regeneration

Many of the UK's worst housing estates do not simply endure material disadvantage but also suffer from poor reputations. They are viewed as 'problem places' that are home to 'problem people'. Some have a local infamy for crime or drug abuse. A few achieve national notoriety after a widely publicised event, such as a particular crime or a period of disorder.

A problem reputation can reinforce or even magnify an estate's material difficulties. The government's Social Exclusion Unit, for example, noted the key role which reputational problems play in exacerbating neighbourhood decline and in eroding communities (Social Exclusion Unit, 2000). There is also evidence that those who live in stigmatised places have a reduced quality of life, directly as a result of negative stereotyping. Wood and Vamplew (1999) note that residents of stigmatised estates in Teeside believed their place of residence reduced the quality of services they received, such as policing and education, and limited their access to jobs and credit.

Stigma is not only a problem for a few isolated neighbourhoods but is also increasingly an issue for the social rented sector in general. Local authority housing in particular went through a turbulent period in the second half of the 1990s with a substantial out-migration from the sector to private renting, where tenants often pay higher rents for poorer housing quality (Cole et al, 1999). Registered social landlords are also becoming concerned that demand is being restricted by the reputation of the sector. For example, housing associations in the North of England believe that the term 'social housing' has to be disowned in order to attract new tenants (National Housing Federation North, 2000). This problem reputation seems to be becoming more embedded, despite the fact that low demand housing occurs in all tenures and is a particular blight in some older owner-occupied neighbourhoods in the North of England (Power and Mumford, 1999).

This report is concerned with the regeneration of primarily social housing estates, which experience a double dose of stigma. The research aimed to explore whether the regeneration process can succeed in tackling this double layer of stigma and whether perceptions of an estate and its people are challenged as a consequence of investment. It assumes that challenging an estate's problem reputation is critical for whether regeneration efforts will be sustainable. Unless problem images are challenged, employers may remain reluctant to employ estate residents, for example, and media coverage may continue to have a negative edge as journalists persist in their expectation of finding problem stories about the estates. Crucially, the estates are unlikely to be places of residential choice for households with options and the lives of estate residents will continue to be blighted by the effects of stigma so that those who can, will continue to leave.

The study focused on three estates:

- *Castle Vale* is a large estate of tower blocks and low rise, system-built houses, built in the late 1960s in the outskirts of Birmingham.
- *Greater Pilton* is a large, fairly central estate in Edinburgh, built in various phases since the 1920s. The built form is mostly walk-up tenements with some system-built properties and a few tower blocks.
- *Meadow Well* is a smallish estate in North Tyneside, well linked to Newcastle and North Shields, comprised largely of traditional terraced housing and cottage flats.

Each has a long-standing poor reputation associated with the history of the neighbourhood in the local area, and each suffers from the more recent stigmatisation of social renting in general. The three cities have different kinds of housing market and development opportunities. For instance, in Edinburgh the housing market is buoyant and the economy growing. In North Tyneside there is a collapsing housing market and economy, whereas Birmingham lies somewhere in the middle of these two extremes. (See Appendix B for a pen portrait of each estate.)

The study was designed to examine attitudes to the estates of employers, journalists and potential and current residents, given their capacity to influence the durability of the regeneration effort. Interviews were carried out with local employers and journalists. Focus groups were conducted with potential and current residents who were, crucially, relatively young and in secure employment; that is, the kinds of people who are leaving or refusing to consider social housing estates, and therefore key targets for regeneration initiatives. Separate focus groups were convened with estate residents and with residents of neighbouring areas who were thinking of moving house. These aimed to explore how residents experienced the estates, what their perceptions of change were and how committed they were to continuing to live there. Focus groups with residents of neighbouring areas aimed to assess their knowledge and perceptions of change on the estates, and whether they would consider moving there. (See Appendix A for more detail on research design and methodology.)

Marketing, regeneration and the social rented sector

A key focus of the report is to consider whether marketing approaches can be useful in countering stigma and, if so, in what ways. Marketing can be thought of as a set of activities that aim to influence people's behaviour, usually their willingness to buy a particular product, but also their willingness to consider specific ideas or to change their attitudes. It is based on the mechanism of *exchange,* which recognises that people will only allow themselves to be influenced if they also derive some benefit from the process. It emphasises the centrality of the customer's perspective, and thus its effectiveness usually depends on an accurate assessment of different consumer needs and preferences; that is, on identifying and understanding different market segments. Marketing approaches can encompass a range of activities including selling products, promotion, branding, customer care and using media and other communication channels effectively (see MacFadyen et al, 1999 for a fuller description).

Marketing has a long history in relation to city boosterism, and the place marketing of whole cities to investors, industry and tourists is now common place (see Ashworth and Voogd, 1995). However, it is a much more recent phenomenon in relation to the social rented sector and in the context of individual neighbourhoods. Some marketing techniques are increasingly used to attract new 'customers' to neighbourhoods and to the sector generally. For example, a number of local authorities, including Manchester, Sheffield and Dundee City Councils, now advertise vacancies in their stock widely and are apparently successful in their attempts to interest people who would not have traditionally expected to qualify for a council house. Housing associations have also embraced marketing as a way in which to attract new applicants, particularly from among the economically active population. One recent manual aims to guide associations in the 'new approach' to generating demand for the sector (National Housing Federation North, 2000). The 'new approach' is based firmly on marketing principles including how to attract customers, how to receive them and how to keep their loyalty. The issue for this report is whether and how marketing can contribute to challenging images of stigmatised estates.

Structure of the report

The remainder of the report is structured as follows.

Chapter 2 explores the attitudes to the case-study estates held by estate residents and residents of nearby areas. It shows that the estates still suffer from significant problems, including a problem reputation, and reveals the sharp differences in perceptions between different groupings of residents and non-residents.

Chapter 3 examines the experiences of estate residents living in stigmatised neighbourhoods, cataloguing the significant impact that stigma has on their lives. It provides evidence of the way in which a continuing stigma can be a handicap to regeneration.

Chapter 4 identifies the range of actors involved in building estate images, and explores how the attitudes and behaviour of private-sector agencies can help to maintain stigma. It argues for the need to enlist their help in challenging negative images.

Chapter 5 continues on the theme of Chapter 4, but focuses on the role of public-sector agencies. It also examines the approaches taken by the regeneration initiatives in the three case-study areas trying to overcome each estate's problem reputation.

Chapter 6 provides some practical suggestions for challenging images. It suggests ways in which different resident and non-resident groupings could be targeted in order to challenge their view of the estates, and provides ideas of how to help other actors adjust their behaviour and become stakeholders in challenging images. It also discusses organisational issues, and regeneration practice more widely.

Chapter 7 concludes with implications both for regeneration policy and, more substantially, for regeneration practice, for tackling negative images.

2

Different perceptions of three estates

This chapter discusses the images of the three case-study estates as portrayed in focus groups with residents and non-residents. It explores their attitudes to the estates and personal priorities for current and future housing needs.

Characteristics of focus group participants

Eight groups were recruited in each area, with all participants members of young, economically secure households. Half of the groups were of estate residents and half non-residents. The groups were separated according to both tenure and their attitude towards living on the estates:

residents who wanted to stay living there or to leave; non-residents who would or would not consider moving there. Recruitment characteristics are illustrated in Figure 1.

Attitudes to the estates

The groups were recruited on the expectation that differences in residence, tenure and snap-shot attitudes to the estates would give rise to groups that differ considerably in their attitudes towards the area, the residents and the potential for change on the estates. A key task was to explore how and why perceptions differ between the groups.

Figure 1: Characteristics of focus group participants

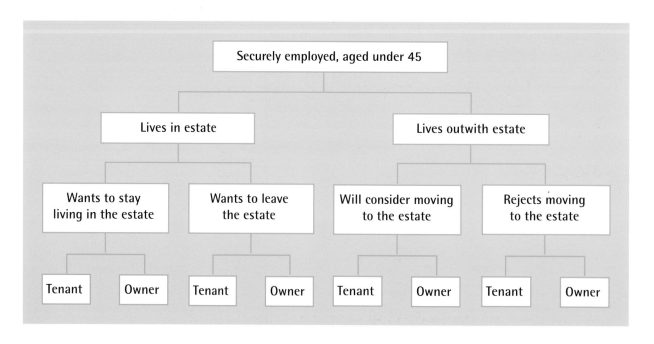

The overall picture

Participants were asked to identify phrases they associate with the estates. Figures 2 to 4, drawn from this data, split the focus groups into four factions based on their attitude towards the estates at the recruitment stage. These illustrate how participants view the estates and show marked differences in attitude.

It should be emphasised that the figures do not illustrate the estates as they are now; rather, they

Figure 2: Perceptions of Castle Vale

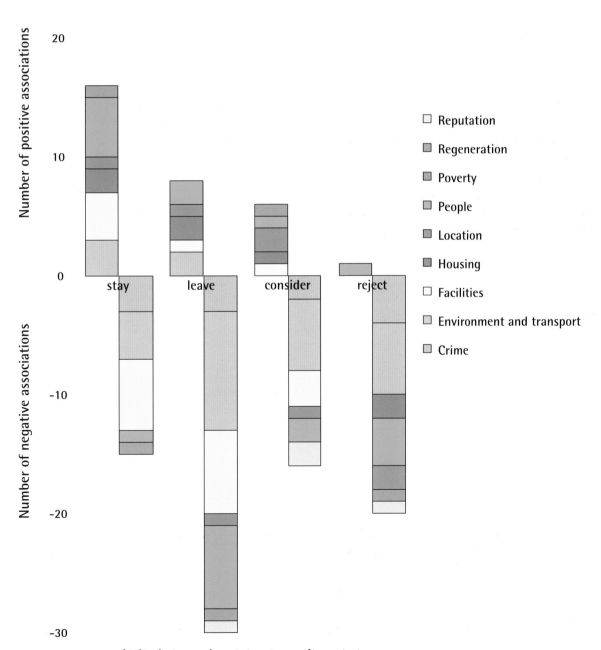

Attitude towards estate at recruitment stage

illustrate what people believe the estates to be. Thus they are a representation of the estates' reputation.

Residents who wanted to continue living on the estates offer the most positive, and least negative, picture of them, while non-residents who will not move there are most negative and least positive. While participants display varying *attitudes*, similar *issues* arise in all groups: for example, some suggest 'housing' is high quality and good value, while others hold the opposite view.

Figure 3: Perceptions of Meadow Well

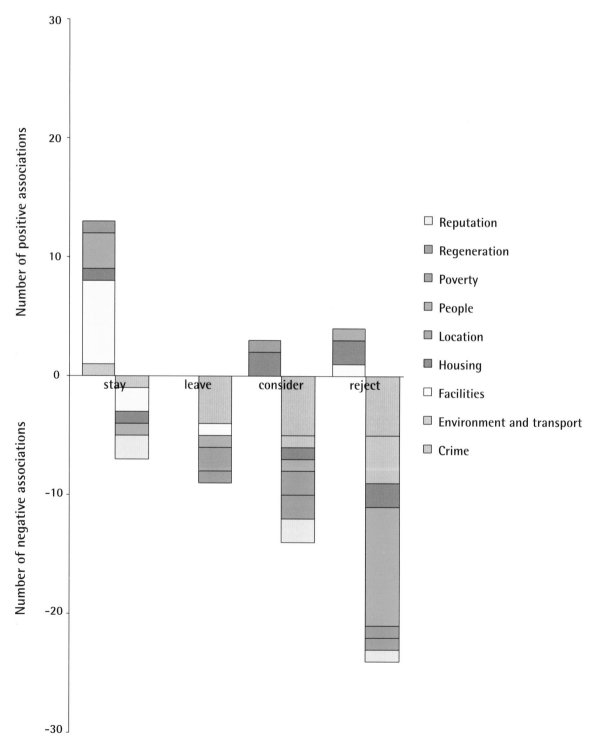

The most common positive associations for residents are the facilities (eg high quality childcare, community buildings) and the people. Yet, alongside crime, facilities also represent the main negative associations for residents (eg lack of shopping, insufficient facilities for young people). Non-residents highlight the environment, crime and the people as negative attributes, and housing and regeneration efforts as positive ones, although some groups volunteered only negative associations initially and needed to be encouraged to identify positive aspects of the estate.

Figure 4: Perceptions of Pilton

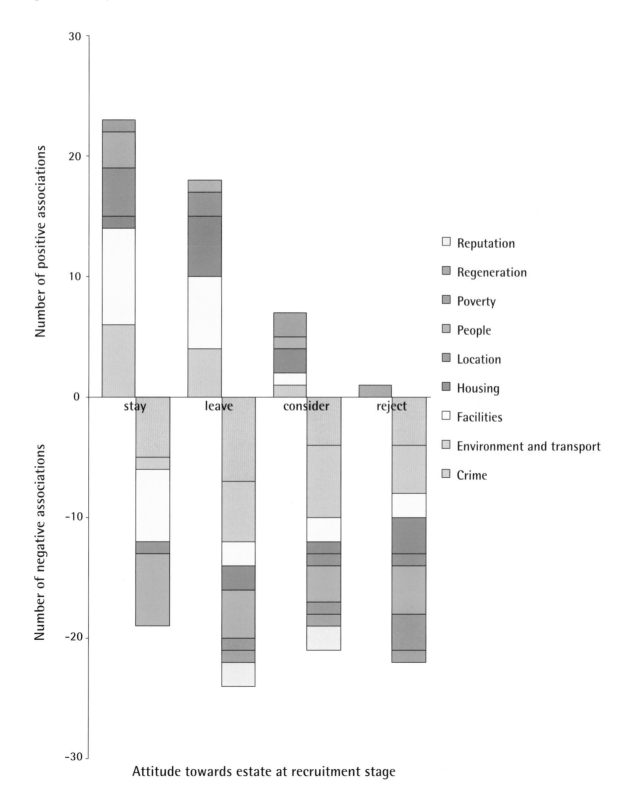

The estates were each selected on the basis of their past problematic image, and an essential first step in the research was to explore whether this persists. Overall, despite regeneration inputs, each estate had a greater number of negative than positive associations. The evidence of the focus groups shows that a problematic image persists in all three estates. Image – termed 'stigma' by residents and 'bad reputation' by outsiders – was raised in all resident and most non-resident groups before they were aware of the research agenda. The substance of this problem image is discussed throughout this chapter and the effects of living with stigma detailed in Chapter 3.

A typology of attitudes

People's attitudes, towards stigmatised estates as towards any other social phenomenon, are complex. Individuals bring their own experiences and political beliefs to their interpretation of life on a stigmatised estate. An individual will often express conflicting opinions on the same subject, apply their knowledge selectively in order to confirm their own prejudices, and will give different credence to different sources of information.

As illustrated by Figures 2 to 4, attitudes vary significantly between groups as far as the same estate is concerned. The split is not as simple as residents and non-residents. A better fit is given by considering whether group members want to stay or leave the estate, and whether they will or will not consider moving there. Tenure is also relevant: owners who want to leave judge the estate more harshly than renters who want to leave; of those who will consider moving to the estate renters are typically more positive than owners.

Figure 5 characterises the attitudes of the focus groups towards the estates. The groups fall into six types, descending from hot, through a lukewarm then cool zone, to very cold.

Using this typology, the remainder of the chapter explores different perceptions of the estates, and the basis of participants' beliefs.

Hot: These are residents who choose to stay. They are typically long-standing residents, well connected within the estate, regularly using its facilities, and are family-oriented. On the basis of these attitudes we can think of these people as *committed residents.*

Warm: Current owners willing to consider the estate are often former residents who are attracted by the price, size and quality of housing. Current renters who are willing to consider the estate typically have fewer connections to it but are aware of changes and are willing to consider buying a first home in the area. We can think of these people as *budding incomers.*

Lukewarm: Renters who want to leave experience regeneration efforts as inconvenient. They report crime and neighbour problems, traffic, noise and dirt, and regard other estate residents as causing its problems. While they expressed a desire to leave the estate when recruited to the research most are not actively trying to move, and they are unlikely to leave the rented sector. On the basis of their dissatisfaction these people are conceived of as *potential leavers.*

Cool: One group, renters who at the recruitment stage were unwilling to consider moving to Pilton, displayed more complex attitudes in the group. They are mainly young professionals, leaning to the Left politically, with little connection to the estate. On the basis of their changing opinions in the course of the focus group, and their reactions to estate publicity, they are termed *doubtful incomers.*

Cold: Owners who want to leave the estate are generally recent incomers who believed change on the estate would be rapid and substantial. They now feel betrayed by the regeneration process and threatened by the social renters around them. They have less community connection than other residents and avoid using estate facilities. This group can be seen as *probable leavers.*

Very cold: Owners who are unwilling to consider the estate are generally young and aspirational professionals. The estate does not have the type of property they are seeking, and is not the type of area they desire. They have little connection to the estate, little awareness of changes, and see no reason to spend time in the area. Similar are the Birmingham and North Shields renters who reject Castle Vale and Meadow Well as places to live. These groups can be termed *improbable incomers.*

Figure 5: Warmth towards the estates: a thermometer

Hot

Committed residents

Budding incomers

Potential leavers

Doubtful incomers

Probable leavers

Improbable incomers

Very cold

The image of the estates

The three estates have broadly the same reputation as impoverished housing estates in general. They are regarded as places of high crime, peopled by the feckless and unemployed. We know this from asking focus group participants what other people think of the estate. This question allows those negatively disposed towards the area to express their own opinions, and those positively disposed to identify the problem reputation:

> "Crime ... vandalism ... drugs ... gangs ... it's dirty ... full of rubbish ... anti-social behaviour ... bad reputation ... boarded-up houses ... children roaming the streets ... stray dogs ... problem families."
> (Improbable incomers, Meadow Well)

But, while the three estates suffer from the general negative image of social housing estates, each also has a specific local reputation. All the Meadow Well groups mentioned the 1991 riots, in Pilton the reputation for drug use was foremost and in Castle Vale the image emphasises crime, particularly car crime.

The image of the people

A key part of the reputation of the estates lies with how the people who live there are perceived. 'The people' was raised in each focus group (see Figures 2 to 4). This had varying meanings: positive attributes such as 'friendly' and 'nice neighbours' are revealed, but also negative attitudes such as 'scumbags' and 'problem families'.

Committed residents represented the estate's population as an asset, and only occasionally a liability:

> "It's just your few bad ones ... the rest are all nice people." (Committed resident, Castle Vale)

There is then a spectrum of attitudes towards the people living on the estates that correlate with the thermometer (Figure 5). Thus, at the other extreme, improbable incomers believe residents are mostly problematic; criminals, workshy and inadequate parents.

Comparisons that participants make with other areas also shed light on the reputation that the estates hold. Places notorious in the popular imagination – the Bronx, East Berlin, Beirut – are drawn on to exemplify what the estates are like, as are other UK estates with a problematic reputation, such as the Gorbals in Glasgow or Manchester's Moss Side:

> "It doesn't seem like part of Western Europe at all really, it is something you would maybe see in Kosovo or something." (Probable leaver, Pilton)

The relevance of image

While almost all groups raised the estate's images as an issue, the relevance that this holds for them differs according to their attitudes to the area. Committed residents and budding incomers see image as a very important problem for the estates. They are aware of, but reject, the reputation of the area, and blame the media and others for creating and perpetuating stereotypes. Committed residents take the image as a personal attack: they believe that the estates used to have problems but have now been improved. The estates are also seen as not as bad as other local areas, and group members are indignant that they are looked down on.

In contrast, improbable and doubtful incomers, and probable and potential leavers believe that reputation and reality coincide. For these groups it makes no sense to ask what causes the reputation. The way to address the reputation is to change the estate and the people. In its extreme form, improbable incomers suggest that nothing, other than flattening the estate, rebuilding it and moving current residents elsewhere, will address the area's reputation:

> "Take all the nice people out and just leave all the dross in and build a brick wall with a cage and a lock and just keep them in there." (Improbable incomer, Meadow Well)

Respondents were asked to consider the estates' reputations separately from what they themselves thought of the areas. There was some evidence that the reputation was changing a little, in particular for budding and doubtful incomers:

> "It used to have a really bad reputation but it's actually changed." (Budding incomer, Pilton)

These groups are conscious of both positive and negative aspects to the estates and attempt to be balanced and fair. Yet there continues to be a tendency for outsiders, even those positively disposed to the estates, to think of the estates as they were, rather than the improved estates. Residents' perceptions of the image of the estates, and the impacts this has on their own lives, is discussed further in the following chapter.

What causes the estates' problems?

Participants' explanations of the estates' problems range from those that are entirely about the people who live there, through explanations that draw on local social policies and labour markets, to those that take in wider structural arguments.

The hot and warm groups are *normalisers*. They argue that everywhere has problems, that most residents are decent and hard working, and that much problematic behaviour by young people is similar to the ways they once behaved themselves. Their explanations for problems concentrate on external influences. There are financial disincentives to leave benefit and find work; low quality services and a lack of investment explain problems with the housing and environment; and a lack of opportunities for bored youngsters create misbehaviour and petty crime. The following quote is a response to a photograph of vandalised housing:

> "Most of the houses were empty when it was like that ... it's not just the people's fault. It's the government's fault as well. The houses are empty, they vandalise them." (Committed resident, Pilton)

Cool, cold and very cold groups are *pathologisers*. They believe that the estate and its residents are problematic. Residents' behaviour and attitudes are felt to be different from their own:

> "A lot of people, they don't want to change anything up there.... I think the younger generation growing up there seem to follow their parents and the parents' attitudes towards life will be dreadful, so they won't change." (Improbable incomer, Castle Vale)

They explain unemployment and the estate's run-down appearance with reference to residents' laziness. Anti-social behaviour is related to inadequate parenting and a general lack of respect for the institutions of social control:

"They've got rubbish from one end of the garden to the other. And if they don't work all day there's nothing stopping them tidying the garden up a little ... to me they lack the basic skills of parenting and cleanliness." (Improbable incomer, Meadow Well)

Is the reputation fixed, changing or changeable?

A key question was whether the reputations of the estates were viewed as changing in response to the regeneration programmes and the attempts of regeneration bodies to tackle image problems.

Table 1 summarises residents' and non-residents' responses to materials displayed during focus groups. While the precise nature of these materials varied in each area, they were selected to offer alternative images of the estates: as run-down and threatening neighbourhoods, and as modernised and safe communities. They included photographs and video-footage taken before regeneration initiatives made substantial change to the estates, and more recent materials that demonstrate changes to the areas. The former were characterised by images of litter, graffiti, derelict housing and unattractive community facilities. The latter typically represented refurbished or newly built housing, clean and tidy streetscapes, and emphasised both community facilities on the estate and neighbouring leisure facilities.

As would be expected, the responses to stimuli follow the group patterns already identified. Committed residents continue to be the most optimistic and defensive about the areas, and their in-depth knowledge of the estates and people makes them well aware of change, and even critical of positive materials that they feel are insufficient in their scope. Improbable incomers are dismissive of the positive materials, regarding them as at best partial and at worst manufactured. These groups, who seldom visit the estates, believe that the negative stimuli are a faithful representation of the area as it is today and that

regeneration inputs have made no discernible difference to the intrinsic nature of the place.

Future prospects of the estates

Residents and non-residents demonstrated different levels of awareness about change on the estates, and offered different visions of the area's likely future. Residents' knowledge of change was drawn largely from personal experience and the information provided by regeneration bodies. Non-residents also had some personal experience of change on the estates, through visiting residents, work, using facilities or just driving past or through the areas. Those with least contact with the estates appeared least aware of change and least willing to consider moving there. However, it is difficult to know whether attitudes towards the areas lead them to avoid it, or whether not visiting the estates means that negative attitudes harden. Both residents and non-residents were more conscious of physical change in the area – in particular high-profile demolition, and new-build owner-occupied areas – than they were of other aspects of the regeneration process.

Tenure diversification, and in particular, the building and sale of owner-occupied houses, is regarded by almost all as a positive sign, which suggests both reputation and the reality is changing. Typically no one expected that these houses would sell. Even committed residents were surprised that others felt confident to invest in the estates and their future, and there was widespread belief that private developers would not take a risk unless they knew there was a market for these houses in these areas.

Committed residents saw regeneration initiatives positively. They believed that the areas had improved, and were optimistic about future change. For them, housing change was the most important and most successful element of the regeneration strategy. While they may have accepted that the reputations were based on the reality of the past, they felt they were not deserved now. Budding incomers were similarly positive about the estates' prospects. Changes on the estates were tangible to them, and they were hopeful for the future. For some, the estates are on the cusp, and another year or two will consolidate change.

Table 1: Summary of the responses to positive and negative images of the estates

Group	Response to positive materials	Response to negative materials
Committed residents	• Stimulated discussion of how the estate has changed and the regeneration process • Seen as partial by some: materials thought to cover only improved bits of the estate, often the new-build owner-occupied housing • Discussion of precisely where the material showed, and debate over whether nearby facilities and neighbourhoods are useful as positive publicity for the estate	• Recognised to be out-of-date and selective • Parts of the estate were like this (perhaps worse) • Estate has improved substantially since then • Outsiders will see the estate like this • Estate was in this state because of council neglect
Budding incomers	• Interested in the materials but needed to see more of the estate • Recognised as partial and selective – showing only improved areas • Stimulated discussion of regeneration initiatives and, in particular, design issues • Little prior awareness of opportunities to buy housing on the estate	• Recognised to be out-of-date and thought to be exaggerating the estate's problems • Estate has improved since then, but regeneration is not complete; some parts remain like this • Estate was in this state because of council neglect and also because of the people who lived there
Potential leavers	• Material seen as partial, showing only the improved areas, not the whole estate	• Recognised to be old materials, but thought to be more recent than committed residents believed • Parts of the estate were like this, but it has improved since • Estate was in this state because of the council's neglect, but some additionally blame the people who lived there and, in particular, drug culture
Doubtful incomers	• Surprised by the materials – not what they expected the estate to be like, impressed by the appearance of the new housing • Wanted to know where in the estate the materials represented, with preference for edge developments • Curious to see images of the wider area and the amenities on the estate • Estate still needs time to consolidate change: probably too much of a risk to move there at present	• Queried the date of the materials; recognised to be up to 10 years old • Parts of the estate were like that • Estate has improved substantially since then • Estate was in this state because of poverty, and group expressed pity for residents
Probable leavers	• Improvements are regarded as superficial/cosmetic: people continue to be the problem • Difficulty with selling houses on the estate – no appreciation or even depreciation • Need to teach people (especially children and teenagers) how to behave • Betrayed by regeneration process; expected outcomes which have failed to materialise	• Materials thought to be only a few years old • Estate now different, but change is very superficial, some parts remain like this • Estate was in this state because of council neglect and unemployment
Improbable incomers	• Highlighted any negative aspects of the material, such as boarded-up housing and design issues • Dubious about how long improvements will last – need to revisit in 12 months to see if change maintained • Houses are more pleasant but the wider environment has not changed, nor have the people who live there • Unwilling to accept neighbouring amenities are evidence of change on the estate • Initiatives to educate and support residents seen as negative, and reinforce image of area • Made respondents more wary of considering adjoining neighbourhoods	• Largely believed to be an accurate representation of the estate today • Any improvements to the estate have been superficial, some parts remain like this • Estate was in this state because of the residents' own behaviour

Potential and probable leavers were not hopeful about the estates' futures. They do not believe that the regeneration process has helped them, or tackled the important problems. Regeneration attempts were regarded as cosmetic and short term, while the root cause of problems, the people, was not tackled. Some felt betrayed, having believed that regeneration would be substantive and rapid. Some leavers have disassociated themselves from the estate so thoroughly that they regarded themselves as having no investment in the future of the area.

Finally, doubtful and improbable incomers regarded the estates as a financial, and sometimes personal, risk. For them, regeneration efforts were not addressing the fundamental problems. They believed that the estates remain an area of high crime and unemployment, and that residents sabotage attempts to change them. These people would not consider the estates unless desperate and could not understand why anyone would choose to live there. They avoid visiting the areas, partly through fear of crime and partly because there is nothing to attract them.

Conclusion

This chapter has demonstrated that each case-study estate continues to hold a poor reputation locally, despite the ongoing process of regeneration. There is some evidence that the reputation is being challenged for some groups of people, but that it persists for a substantial part of the population. A critical finding is that it is not appropriate to talk of *the image* of an estate. Rather there are *fractured images*, with people's opinions differing depending on their mechanisms for interpreting the world, and their personal priorities and belief systems, as well as the experiences that they have had. The question for regeneration initiatives is: can negative attitudes be challenged and how? This issue is returned to in Chapter 6.

3

Living with stigma: impacts on life chances

Introduction

This chapter describes the multiple ways that residents of stigmatised estates believe they are discriminated against. It reveals that the reputation of the area is critical to the lives of residents and argues that this should be a key concern of the regeneration process. While not all residents claim that the reputation of the area they live in has a direct impact on all aspects of their lives, all reported that stigma affects their life in some way. The weight of their evidence points to lives that are impoverished by the operation of stigma.

The chapter does not attempt to corroborate residents' claims. While some of the impacts cannot be measured, and others are disputed by service providers and employers (see Chapters 4 and 5, and note that further research in this area is planned), it is residents' experiences and their perceptions of prejudice that are important here.

Economic impacts of stigma

Residents believe they are economically disadvantaged by living on the estates in a number of ways. Access to employment is believed to be damaged by employers' preconceptions of estate residents, and, for those in employment, experiences at work are coloured by stigma. Many have experienced either refusal or higher costs of home and car insurance, and of credit. For homeowners, buying and selling property on the estates was problematic.

Employment

All of the research participants are employed or live with an employed partner. Their views on the

impacts of stigma on residents' chances of finding employment must therefore be interpreted with the knowledge that these people, with a work history and, presumably, effective job search strategies, are among the most employable estate residents. If they experience the effects of stigma, residents who are currently unemployed, are unskilled or have no work history are likely to face even greater difficulties.

There are a number of reasons why accessing work is likely to be particularly difficult for residents of the case study estates: the average lower level of qualifications, decline in demand for unskilled manual labour, and problems with travel to and from places where work is situated. This research additionally highlights residents' claims that the estates' reputations affects their ability to find work:

> "I applied to any job that was sort of local, within bus reach. And I've never got so far as an interview and I don't know if it was, but I always wondered if it was about Castle Vale on my address on my application." (Committed resident, Castle Vale)

Others believed that the reputation of their senior school was an additional barrier to their finding work:

> "It's like Craigroyston School. If they see that on your application.... You just expect a negative response." (Potential leaver, Pilton)

Those who have not themselves experienced the impacts of stigma in finding employment know of others who have. Most often this involved friends and acquaintances who have been rejected on the basis of their addresses, but on occasion participants have seen their managers reject other estate residents:

> "My pal went for a job in [national company] and when she said she was living in Muirhouse, they just took one look at the application – and that was it. And she was qualified to do the job and everything." (Potential leaver, Pilton)

Insurance

Some residents reported that they could not get house contents or car insurance, while others believed the area's reputation meant they were being charged higher premiums than would otherwise be the case. Residents perceived premiums by postcode as unfair and discriminatory:

> "My premiums went up ... there's been no damage but because we're in NE29. I've had no trouble over the last year, it's still gone up." (Committed resident, Meadow Well)

Access to insurance was a concern of many, and is clearly critical to households with lower incomes, less able to cover emergencies through their own resources. Some residents felt that obtaining adequate insurance was now easier because the estate was improving, but others reported a continuing problem.

Credit and financial services

Residents also reported both being refused credit or forced to use higher cost credit. A number who had sought to spread costs through hire purchase, for example, had been rejected. Some had worked around the problem by using a relative's address as a cover. Others responded by always paying cash and now referred to this as a deliberate budgeting strategy:

> "We've given the postcode and they don't want to know ... it just meant you had to pay cash anyway. And that's what we've always done." (Committed resident, Castle Vale)

Similarly, some who would like to have operated a catalogue found their addresses were blacklisted. One woman's existing catalogue

company had rejected her when she moved onto the Pilton estate from elsewhere in Edinburgh.

Problems in accessing credit through mainstream sources meant residents sought credit through routes that offered less advantageous terms. Residents were resentful of the additional costs arising from high interest and charges:

> "[They] charge extortionate prices and they can get away with it because they're the only debt company that will accept people on the estate." (Potential leaver, Meadow Well)

Buying and selling houses

The impact of reputation on the operation of the local housing market is of particular interest given its role in creating and maintaining economically mixed and sustainable communities.

Problems in selling houses were reported in both Castle Vale and Pilton (no Meadow Well owners who wanted to leave were involved in the research), but appear to be most severe in Pilton despite Edinburgh's booming property market. Residents of both new-build property and right-to-buy housing reported prolonged periods on the market, and advice from estate agents to drop the asking price:

> "If I put my house on the market for £15,000 I still wouldn't get anybody over my doorstep to look at it ... I was at the estate agent a couple of weeks ago who asked me to bring the house price down." (Probable leaver, Pilton)

A number of Pilton residents had had their houses on the market for substantial periods of time. Others, seeing the difficulties of friends and neighbours, had not put their house on the market despite their desire to leave and reported feeling trapped. Homeowners in all three estates reported that their house's value was depressed by the reputation of the area.

Those wanting to buy homes on the estates also face difficulties believed to be driven by the area's reputation. Two issues arise: surveyors' valuation reports, which allude to the area's reputation and likely difficulties with resale; and mortgage lenders unwilling to offer mortgages in the area.

This was as true for discrete new-build schemes as for former council homes:

> "It had on the [surveyor's] report that it was right next to Meadow Well – 'a poorly managed housing scheme which will never change from the notorious Meadow Well'." (Committed resident, Meadow Well)

Table 2 summarises the varying economic impacts of stigma on residents' lives, and introduces some of the coping strategies they employ.

Stigma and relationships

This section discusses how stigma affects relationships with friends, relatives and colleagues, and how it impacts on meeting new people:

> "No matter where you go, if you mention where you come from, you're classed as muck." (Committed resident, Pilton)

Friends' and relatives' attitudes to the estates

Residents who had moved onto the estates from other local areas reported their friends and relatives expressing surprise, even horror, that

Table 2: Economic impacts of stigma and residents' responses

	Insurance and credit	Selling and buying houses	Employment
Expression of stigma	• Refusal of insurance/credit and/or higher costs of these products for residents	• Depressed house prices and difficulties with professional services offered	• Discrimination when applying for work
Impact on residents	• Examples of residents living without insurance or paying more than they felt was reasonable • Affordability is a key concern and residents are unlikely to be able to cover the risk of having no insurance • Potential danger of using less reputable sources of credit	• Examples of residents' houses being on the market for prolonged periods • Feeling trapped on the estate • Difficulties being accepted for a mortgage	• Knowledge of others struggling to find work (but little direct experience)
Coping strategies employed by residents	• Refusal of some forms of credit tackled by using 'care of' addresses • Paying cash • Residents reported using higher cost credit rather than lower cost options such as credit unions	• Little opportunity for residents to work around this problem; however, there was an example of residents using the media to put pressure on mortgage lenders • There was also an indication that residents might try to sell their home through informal networks rather than professional routes	• Being creative with addresses given on application forms • Questioning the practices of particular employers • Challenging individual managers

they would consider a move to Pilton, Castle Vale or Meadow Well. A move to the estates was regarded as the worst of luck or poor judgement, and people often actively tried to prevent the move:

> "Each one of my friends said 'You can't take a house in Muirhouse, there's no way you can take a house in Muirhouse'." (Committed resident, Pilton)

While some friends and relatives changed their minds about the estate as they came to know it, for others the passing of time has not changed their perceptions:

> "They've still got the same attitude as when I came over here 11 years ago. That's not changed, even though I can say we've got new flats now." (Committed resident, Castle Vale)

In particular the estates' reputations as places of high crime meant relationships could become strained, with family members reducing contact because of their fear of crime:

> "I've seen none of my family for months because they just won't come on here." (Committed resident, Castle Vale)

Colleagues' attitudes towards the estates

Residents reported that they were regularly faced with both overt and more subtle expressions of stigma from colleagues and managers. These were experienced by residents in all types of employment, including shop work, office jobs and manual labour. The attitudes of colleagues was felt to be an important way in which residents are stigmatised:

> "Senior management have still got a stigma against Meadow Well … sometimes it's just a jibe when you're in a staff meeting but it's always brought up…. You've just got to mention the name and you get loads of stick." (Committed resident, Meadow Well)

> "They're at it all day long when they find out where you live. At work. Just all their little snide comments." (Committed resident, Pilton)

Some residents, anticipating the reactions that colleagues and managers might have, attempted to avoid the issue entirely. Others will challenge these attitudes:

> "Where I've worked before, when you say to people [you live in] West Pilton, somebody will say, 'That's where all the druggies come from' … I said, 'I work beside you, why say that'." (Committed resident, Pilton)

Meeting new people

Residents felt that the estates' reputations went before them, and affected both the way that new people responded to them and the opinions of acquaintances who found out where they lived:

> "It's sort of, 'You can't be a very nice person', if you're off Castle Vale." (Committed resident, Castle Vale)

'Where do you live?', is a common early question on meeting new people, but for residents of stigmatised estates there is fear that they will be judged and found wanting. Residents vary in their strategies for dealing with this, but many mislead others about where they live:

> "People make judgements … I just say actually 'North West Edinburgh', because that includes Crammond area as well. Because I feel really uncomfortable saying to people 'West Pilton'." (Probable leaver, Pilton)

The general pattern is that the residents who wanted to move from the estates tried to avoid the question, felt embarrassed or ashamed, and lied on occasion. In avoiding the question they would usually make a vague geographical reference or refer to nearby more prestigious neighbourhoods. Conversely, those who wanted to stay living in the areas were more likely to adopt an honest policy, expecting to need to confront the prejudice of others when they give their addresses. The occasions when they did try to avoid naming the estates were typically when applying for work.

There are also examples of stigma affecting embryonic relationships with new people:

Table 3: Stigma and relationships: impacts and responses

	Friends and family	Colleagues	New acquaintances	Strangers
Expression of stigma	• Critical of move to estate • Reducing contact	• Disparaging comments • Some evidence that residents are judged by different standards	• Assumptions about the type of people residents are	• Disparaging comments in public places, not addressed to residents
Impact on residents	• Reduces pleasure of a new home • Damage to relationships over prolonged periods • Feelings of shame and failure	• Either ground down or made angry • Some fears that problems at work will be blamed on them • Feeling uncomfortable around colleagues	• New relationships put under strain • Some examples of new acquaintances rejecting residents • Some examples of children fighting	• Either ground down or made angry
Coping strategies employed by residents	• Accept their fears and avoid the need for them to visit • Make estate an off-limits topic of conversation/avoid conflict • Introduce them to the estate, facilities and residents • Direct challenge	• Avoid telling colleagues where they live, at least until the relationship is stronger • Ignore comments • Public affirmation of connection to estate and direct challenge • Question source of their knowledge	• Avoid telling others where they live, at least until the relationship is stronger • Direct challenges to their assumptions	• Ignore comments • Public affirmation of connection to estate and direct challenge • Question source of their knowledge

"You can chat a lass up and as soon as they ask, 'Where are you from?', 'North Shields', 'Oh whereabouts?', 'Meadow Well', 'Ugggh'. And they're away." (Potential leaver, Meadow Well)

Residents also faced expressions of stigma from strangers who they haven't even met, for example, overhearing disparaging comments in public places:

"You're in the Metro and you hear people talking about Meadow Well and going on about the state of the place and the state of the people." (Committed resident, Meadow Well)

Table 3 summarises the varying impacts of stigma on personal relationships, as well as some of the coping strategies used by residents.

Impacts of stigma on service delivery

Residents argued that service providers held a low opinion of the estates and of the people who lived there. This, they believe, means they receive lower quality services than others in the wider area. This section discusses residents' criticisms of the services provided by both the public and private sector.

A variety of council services (and, in Castle Vale, HAT services) were criticised by residents. Complaints were about the speed, quality or frequency of services, and the attitudes of staff who delivered them. Distinct from wider dissatisfaction with public services, it was felt that living in a stigmatised estate meant services were delivered at a lower standard.

Three areas in particular were important to respondents: the repair and maintenance service of landlords; regeneration work on the estates; and maintenance including landscaping, cleansing service and refuse collection.

Residents talked about their frustrations with landlords when repairs were needed:

"They don't care as long as they are getting the money for the rent. They are not interested. If you want a repair done it takes six months." (Potential leaver, Pilton)

The maintenance of public areas, and collection of rubbish was felt to be poor on all three estates:

"When I was walking round the other day, there was a lot of rubbish and overgrown grass all over the place. They don't do it like they used to and when they do it, they leave it everywhere." (Committed resident, Castle Vale)

A further way in which landlords could be seen to discriminate against an estate is through allocations policies that place 'problem' tenants in these areas, showing a lack of concern for residents. Focus-group participants believed this happened and were angered by it:

"I went to see my property ... she said to me ... 'This is where we put problem families' ... I said, 'What do you mean? I'm not a problem family'. She said, 'Oh, it just means families with problems'. So I was put in what they called a problem area ... they actually had a policy of putting 'problem' families on Castle Vale." (Probable leaver, Castle Vale)

There are police stations on Meadow Well and Castle Vale, and immediately adjacent to Pilton. However, residents are critical of the policing service they receive. Two complaints are made: the need for a higher profile police presence and slow response rates. In particular, police are thought to prioritise other areas and to regard crime on the estates as less serious than crime elsewhere. Police are felt to be offhand with residents, and there is a sense that residents should be used to crime:

"When I got burgled, he [police officer] actually came into my house and he said, 'I feel very sorry, I've just come from ... a woman there has just been broke into and had all her Christmas stuff pinched'. And I thought, hang on, I've just had all my stuff ... the whole house. [But] I'm from Castle Vale, so you've just got to expect it." (Committed resident, Castle Vale)

There are also examples of residents finding it harder to employ private sector companies to carry out work for them or make other private transactions. For example:

"Same with repair places. You 'phone up to get your telly repaired, they refuse to come out 'cos of the area." (Potential leaver, Pilton)

> "When I first got a car [the shop] had on its window that there was a garage for rent ... I went over and asked if I could have the garage and pay for it. No, because I lived other side of the road." (Committed resident, Meadow Well)

Taxis may be of particular importance to car-less estate residents both for regular chores such as shopping and occasional journeys such as hospital visits. As the authors discovered through personal experience while conducting fieldwork, the quality of service provided by taxi and mini-cab companies may also be affected by the estates' reputations. Respondents described giving a false destination when ordering a taxi to take them to the estates, and were aware of particular local companies that would not pick up on the estates:

> "Some taxi services just don't want to know if you say Castle Vale.... 'Well, it's out of our area'. And they're just up the road." (Potential leaver, Castle Vale)

At the time of the research, Castle Vale and Pilton were undertaking major remodelling and renovation of shopping facilities. In both areas residents could remember when shopping facilities were more varied and of higher quality. Residents did not see shopping on the estates as a leisure activity; rather it was for essentials only, and often a last resort:

> "You go into [supermarket] and you still can't get the stuff that you're wanting ... half the shelves are emptied and you go and complain ... and it's 'They're not getting any stock in the now'. And I thought, 'Well, are we supposed to all starve?'." (Potential leaver, Pilton)

Residents did not make a link between the quality of shopping facilities and the estates' reputation. There was no suggestion that lower quality shopping was created by a poor image. However, some did see a link between the quality of shopping and the message that the estate sends to residents and non-residents. There was a belief that lower quality shopping added to the estates' poor image, and that improved facilities will start to change the image:

> "Once the shops are done ... you're going to find a lot more people who're going to say hang on, they're cleaning it up, everything's getting sorted. A lot of people I think are going to want to come back on ... as soon as it's done." (Committed Resident, Castle Vale)

Table 4 summarises the impacts of stigma on how services are delivered to estate residents, and some of the coping strategies residents employ.

Table 4: Service delivery and stigma: impacts and responses

	Service quality	Attitudes of frontline staff
Expression of stigma	• Lower quality services, delivered less frequently • Higher costs, less choice	• Disparaging comments • Less effort in providing service
Impact on residents	• Less pleasant environment to live in • Anger, particularly towards public sector services	• Anger • Humiliation
Coping strategies employed by residents	• Complaints to organisation • Avoiding estate-based services (such as shops) • Private initiative (such as cleaning public areas themselves)	• Some evidence of direct challenges to individuals

Experiencing the media

Residents believed that the majority of media coverage was negative in tone and content, and many felt their estate was unfairly treated. Some argued that the news agenda was misplaced:

> "You 'phone the press up and you say to them … 'So and so has raised that much for the Vale and they've done this for the Vale'…. They'll go, 'Yes, well, that's not really news'. Yet it is. I mean it just goes to show you what a community we've got." (Committed resident, Castle Vale)

Others argued that when something did happen in the area, the prominence the story was given and the overall treatment by the press, was driven by the estate's reputation:

> "The area actually draws more media attention when something does happen … something bad." (Committed resident, Pilton)

Many residents regarded media coverage of the estate as partial, and exaggerated. They accused journalists of using out-of-date images of the estate to illustrate social problems current in the wider area, and argued that new photographs and film footage were selective in what they showed.

Residents also believed that the media manufactured stories and images to fit popular preconceptions about the estates. In Meadow Well the media were believed to have paid children to smash windows; in Pilton one resident's son had been bought chips by the camera crew who filmed him, creating a story about local teenagers eating junk food; and in Castle Vale a resident believed that the newspaper had doctored a photograph of the estate:

> "They superimposed a tower block just behind those new houses. Now there isn't a tower block. There never has been one and there never will be one. They superimposed that because that is what everybody's view is of Castle Vale."
> (Probable leaver, Castle Vale)

Residents are extremely sensitive to the use of evocative phrases that are repeatedly applied to by the media to the area in which they live. Such common phrases include: run down, deprived, riot-torn, notorious, crime-ridden. Considerable anger was displayed at the use of such terms, which create a negative tone while describing something praiseworthy:

> "This is media words isn't it? Use the English language in the way they put us down." (Committed resident, Castle Vale)

The media's desire to contextualise stories means that no report of the estates is ever neutral. Residents note that even positive press will typically have a paragraph explaining what makes the estate newsworthy: its problems and its reputation.

The emotional impacts of stigma

This section focuses on how stigma makes residents feel, and how they respond to that. Many residents believed that stigma extends into virtually all aspects of their lives, and Figures 2 to 4 summarised their attempts to lessen its everyday impacts. Here we concentrate on emotional responses to stigma.

The estates' reputations have an emotional impact felt by virtually all. Exposure to stigma makes residents feel angry, hurt, and upset. Others referred to being made to feel like 'second-class citizens'. Some took the reputation of the area as an insult to themselves and other residents. Others believed that many residents deserved the reputation, but felt it was undeserved in their cases and resented being considered the same:

> Robert: "You can see it in their faces as soon as you mention – I'm from the Meadow Well."
>
> Researcher: "How does that make you feel?"
>
> Lucy: "Horrible."
> (Potential leavers, Meadow Well)

Their responses can be broadly categorised as:

- *Challenge:* residents strongly identified with the estates and rejected their reputations;
- *Fatalism:* residents may have rejected the reputations of the estates, or at least its application to themselves, but felt powerless to change perceptions;
- *Avoidance:* employed at different times by

residents, in situations when it was easier or wiser not to 'come out'.

- *Acceptance:* those who did not identify with the estates and believed the reputations to be valid.

For some, their anger caused them to challenge in their view, the undeserved reputations. These people complained to newspapers, wrote pointed notes to employers and argued with strangers in defence of the estates:

> "Somebody who's never been to the Vale, doesn't know anybody off the Vale, they've just heard what a reputation it's had in the past and automatically you get that – 'scum'. And that really irritates me 'cos I go to work every day, I earn my money, I pay my rent, I don't owe anybody anything." (Committed resident, Castle Vale)

These people also defend their community, for example, by portraying people from nearby areas as lazy and bad housekeepers. The implication is that these outsiders have not earned the right to judge residents. They are also normalisers, arguing that the stigmatised behaviour of residents is no different from the behaviour of others: all children swear and eat junk food; all adults were once teenagers who would gather outside the local off-licence.

Others adopted a fatalistic attitude. The man quoted below is currently employed but was convinced that stigma had damaged job opportunities in the past. He is now somewhat resigned. Convinced that he can say and do nothing to change attitudes, his approach has become:

> "It's their loss. That's the way I look at it." (Committed resident, Meadow Well)

Finally, some residents appeared to have internalised the estates' negative image. These people, who believe that the reputation is largely deserved, are less likely to challenge or to ignore expressions of stigma. They are embarrassed and ashamed to be residents of the estate and avoid others finding out when they can:

> "It makes you feel like the down and outs that run about here." (Potential leaver, Pilton)

The research was not designed to explore whether living in a stigmatised area lowers people's aspirations and expectations of life, but this would not seem to be an unreasonable assumption. We would speculate that constant repetition from varied sources of the message that you are different, lesser, and unlikely to succeed, coupled with rejection from other people and organisations, would eventually lead to many people losing the desire to prove them wrong. Some evidence pointing to this is offered by resident parents who do not want their children to grow up on the estate:

> "My kids have got no chance if they stay here. The only chance they've got is going to jail if I stay on this estate." (Potential leaver, Meadow Well)

Conclusion: how stigma is revealed

The chapter has explored the impacts of stigma on estate residents' lives. The focus has been on the effects of stigma, rather than the processes by which stigma operates. Generally for jobs, service quality and economic issues, the perceptions of outsiders are hidden or disguised. For example, organisations do not respond to requests for information, load premiums, or advise against purchasing property on the estates in a way which is presented as neutral rather than the operation of prejudice. For this reason, as with other concerns regarding equal opportunities, it would be very difficult to prove that such prejudice applied in any one case. However, the weight of evidence, coupled with some known indiscretions by, for example, employers and surveyors, suggests that the residents' perceptions of prejudice by such institutions are likely to be grounded in at least partial reality.

Where stigma is expressed in the relationships between estate residents and people living elsewhere it is typically more overt. Residents have reported dismissive and critical comments, and even where nothing is said they may detect an underlying judgement being made. Located between these two types of stigma is the delivery of services to estate residents by frontline staff who may well translate their negative attitudes towards the areas into words and actions.

Clearly, despite the massive regeneration investments into the three estates over a sustained period, and visible change to the areas, their bad reputations remain. This is translated into a stigma that impoverishes all residents' lives in some way, and is felt by some residents to impact on all areas of their lives. Residents are not passive and have developed some creative strategies for coping with these expressions of stigma and lessening the impacts that stigma has on their lives. However, these responses do not resolve the problem. From their testimony we can argue that challenging images must be a priority for regeneration initiatives if the investment is to have the desired lasting consequences. The following chapter explores the role of different agencies in perpetuating a negative reputation. Ways of tackling the problem are identified in Chapter 6.

4

Building estate images: key actors and activities

Introduction

Estate regeneration is a long and complex process. As previous chapters show, despite significant change on all three estates, outsiders' perceptions of the estates seem to lag behind the process of change and residents continue to be stigmatised. The purpose of this chapter is to explore why this is the case. It analyses the attitudes and activities of some key actors in the regeneration process and considers how these shape problem reputations. It focuses mainly on private-sector actors and on the media, while Chapter 5 explores the role of public services and regeneration initiatives.

Understanding estate images: a framework

It is important to identify the range of actors involved in building images of estates and their different contributions to this process. Table 5 illustrates selected actors' involvement in building images. These contributions can be thought of as three distinct processes:

- *responding to images:* activities and behaviours that are simple reactions to an estate's image. Such responses could be immediate reactions to specific stimuli or more gradual adjustment of behaviour to take account of the background reputation. Deliberate challenges to images are not ascribed to this heading;
- *shaping images:* activities that contribute to the nature of images created or sustained, positively or negatively. These are likely to be *unconscious* rather than deliberate, and so any contribution is inadvertent;

- *challenging images:* activities which are done *deliberately* in order to influence, manage or challenge perceptions of the estate. Challenging images can both be strategic or *ad hoc* and may address either individual images, or the general background noise of a problem reputation.

Table 5 describes the authors' view of the typical level of involvement of each actor in each activity.

Estate residents, for example, are argued to be involved in all three processes in the Table 5. Their main activity is shaping images because their characteristics, attitudes and behaviour unconsciously contribute to creating and maintaining perceptions of the estate. A secondary activity for this group is challenging images. As Chapter 3 showed, some residents will deliberately try to influence perceptions of their estates, perhaps by disputing with detractors. Finally, estate residents also respond to images. For example, they may internalise negative images leading to lowered expectations or even decide to leave the estates.

The key point about Table 5 is that it shows that the activities of the actors are not evenly divided between 'responding to', 'shaping' and 'challenging images'. This uneven distribution provides a crucial clue as to why the stigma of housing estates can persist throughout and beyond regeneration. While most actors are involved in responding to or shaping images, few are involved in challenging images. Moreover, only two have this as their main role; community activists and community-based media. There are, therefore, relatively few resources devoted to managing perceptions of the estates, compared with those expended in shaping and reacting to

Table 5: Building estate images: actors and roles

Actors	Responding to images	Shaping images	Challenging images
		Roles performed	
Estate residents	✓	✓✓✓	✓✓
Community activists	-	✓✓✓	✓✓✓
Residents of neighbouring areas	✓✓✓	-	-
Regeneration initiatives	✓	✓✓✓	✓✓
Public Services			
Housing organisations	✓✓	✓✓✓	✓
Cleansing services	✓✓✓	✓✓	-
Schools on estate	✓	✓✓✓	✓✓
Police service	✓✓✓	✓✓	✓
Leisure services	✓✓	✓✓✓	-
Private Services			
Estate agents	✓✓	✓✓✓	-
Property surveyors	✓✓✓	✓✓	-
Housing developers	✓✓	✓✓	✓✓
Insurance companies	✓✓✓	✓✓	-
Other finance (eg banks, credit)	✓✓✓	✓✓	-
Retail (especially supermarkets)	✓✓✓	✓✓	✓
Estate-based employers	✓✓✓	✓✓	-
Other local employers	✓✓✓	-	-
Commercial media	✓✓	✓✓✓	-
Community-based media	-	✓✓	✓✓✓

Key: ✓✓✓ main activity; ✓✓ secondary activity; ✓ lesser activity; – no activity

images. As Chapter 5 argues, regeneration initiatives play an important role, although this is not their main activity and, crucially, many public-sector service providers do not, or barely, participate.

Table 5 shows a number of actors for whom 'shaping perceptions' is their main role including: estate residents, community activists, regeneration initiatives, estate agents and commercial media. These different actors can have contrasting interests in relation to the estate. While estate residents, community activists and regeneration initiatives have a considerable stake in shaping perceptions in positive ways, estate agents and the commercial media do not. The media, for

example, may have a interest in problem images that are seen as 'newsworthy'.

Thus, two issues arise from the distribution of the various actors across these processes. First, there is a need to maximise the range of actors and resources involved in challenging images. Second, those actors involved in shaping images should have the future of the estate as their main interest. Simply, there is a need to maximise the number of stakeholders in the estate's future in the 'shaping images' column, and to minimise the number of deliberate or accidental saboteurs.

The rest of the chapter focuses on the roles currently played by private-sector services, employers and the media in sustaining stigmatising images. Chapter 5 examines the contributions of public sector agencies and regeneration initiatives.

Private-sector services and estate images

The study did not involve direct interviews with representatives of private-sector services on their contribution to estate imaging. Nonetheless the research did provide some initial evidence of the kinds of roles played by these actors. Further research on this theme is being planned at the time of writing. The discussion begins by examining the role of estate agents, before turning to the roles of other actors.

Estate agents

The experiences of estate residents buying and selling property on the estate were explored in Chapter 3. Residents felt that they were being short-changed by estate agents, believing they undervalued their homes or unfairly alluded to the estate's problem reputation. However, among non-resident participants in the focus groups, there was virtually unanimous distrust of estate agents. Interestingly this was because they believed that agents were only interested in making a sale and would therefore try to sell any property to a prospective purchaser:

> "They just want to make money out of you probably and I really don't think they would have your best interests at heart. They would have their own." (Doubtful incomer, Pilton)

In particular, estate agents were thought unlikely to forewarn them of any neighbourhood problems:

> "If it's a bad area, they're not gonna say, 'oh yeah its terrible, I wouldn't live there'." (Improbable incomer, Castle Vale)

So, neither residents nor non-residents believed that estate agents would act in their particular interests, although they anticipated diametrically opposed behaviours. Clearly, both cannot be right. Discovering who is, is important for understanding the role of estate agents in building images and contributing to the success of the

regeneration process. If residents are right, estate agent behaviour has the potential to undermine regeneration efforts, because they are reacting to and helping to maintain the estate's stigma. If non-residents are right, their behaviour will contribute to the success of regeneration, by helping to attract new residents.

In order to explore this issue, the research team carried out a 'mystery shopper' telephone survey, posing as a potential homebuyer in each of the three cities. Would homes for sale on the estates be undersold by estate agents who continued to stigmatise the estates? Or, conversely, would they simply try to sell these properties as they would any others, without caveats about possible difficulties?

The researcher posed as a first-time buyer moving to the city to take up employment close to each case-study estate. The 'prospective buyer' had two stipulations in terms of the kind of property they wished to purchase, both designed to identify them as a potential purchaser for the case-study estates:

- the need to find a cheaper than average property;
- the wish to live within walking distance of their place of work, or in an area with good public transport links to their employment.

The survey findings confirmed the fears of residents and suggested that estate agents were continuing to stigmatise the estates. For example, in only one of the cities, Birmingham, did any estate agent actually suggest properties from the case-study estate. If available properties are not suggested to clients, the pool of potential purchasers is both artificially constrained and prices are likely to be depressed. This has the potential to undermine regeneration efforts.

Given that estate agents did not generally suggest the estates, the researcher was forced to ask about the availability of properties on the estates. Many estate agents were obviously surprised to hear the estates suggested as areas the client was considering. Reactions ranged from nervous coughs, sniggers and even laughs as well as immediate forthright advice not to consider the area. Indeed, many Edinburgh and North Shields agents attempted to dissuade the 'client' from thinking of Pilton or Meadow Well. This was not the case with North Birmingham agencies who did not usually offer such discouragement. Castle

Vale has a longer history of owner-occupation than the others (one part of the estate was originally built for sale) and the fact that estate agents have longer experience of operating there may explain this difference.

Actual deterrence strategies were many and varied. For example, some warned about the difficulties of reselling, perhaps without realising that such a prophecy is likely to be self-fulfilling:

> "The revamped ones are flats but I know from previous experience, because we've marketed in that area, that they're very difficult to resell. You would have to be prepared that you're not going to sell one of them straight away." (Estate agent, Edinburgh)

There were explicit warnings about the estate's reputation:

> "It does have a bad reputation, but it's getting better now. It's not as bad as it was. But I think that it will always hold that stigma. A bad housing estate never really gets rid of its stigma." (Estate agent, North Shields)

Again, the agents appear unaware of their own role in maintaining the stigma! Or, some agents 'alerted' the client to the problems of the estate, by pointing up that it was home to households who rent from the council:

> "There's a lot of tenants there and it doesn't get the best reputation.... They did knock down some of the council houses and build some residential." (Estate agent, Edinburgh)

Further strategies for dissuading purchasers included agents saying that they wouldn't live there, warnings of security risks or simply offering properties that which did not meet their client's stipulations.

A number of these deterrence strategies are illustrated in the transcript of the conversation between a member of the research team and an Edinburgh estate agent reproduced in the box opposite.

Transcript of a telephone conversation between a prospective house buyer and an estate agent selling property in the Pilton area

The house buyer is a female first-time buyer about to take up employment in a hospital near to the estate. She would like to live within walking distance of her place of work, or somewhere with good public transport links to the hospital. She can afford a property valued up to £40,000, which represents a limited budget in the Edinburgh housing market. Up until this point in the conversation, the estate agent has not volunteered Pilton as a possible area to consider, despite its proximity to the hospital.

> Researcher: "I was told that the only area I would be able to afford nearby would be the Pilton or Muirhouse area."
>
> Estate Agent: "Well I wouldn't recommend that. No certainly not. You're obviously young, and are you single?"
>
> Researcher: " I'll be living on my own, yes."
>
> Estate Agent: "I wouldn't recommend that, no."
>
> Researcher: "So from a safety point of view?"
>
> Estate Agent: "Uh huh."
>
> Researcher: "I did wonder why he said, 'You'd be lucky to find anything except there'."
>
> Estate Agent: "Pilton and these places, they're.... It's a dreadful thing to say, but if you're asking my advice, no, because they're drug users et cetera. There are obviously parts of it which are not bad, but I wouldn't recommend any young female to be there."
>
> Researcher: "I was going to go and look at it myself."
>
> Estate Agent: "No, you wouldn't want to. There are a lot of high-rise flats, you'd probably get a high-rise flat there for 35, 40,000 but you wouldn't want to stay there. You can possibly find somewhere like the lower end of Gorgie, Dalry, but it's not as close to the Western as you'd like to be...."

The discussion moved on to prices in the housing market in Edinburgh in general before concluding:

> Estate Agent: "But I certainly wouldn't recommend Pilton.... We're actually about to put one back on that's in West Pilton, but I'm sorry I wouldn't recommend it to you. What you need to do is to speak to someone who knows the areas, and knows the areas to sort of steer you clear of."

The agent has at least one property to sell in the area, yet marshalls a wide range of techniques to repel an interested client. It is assumed that the client is young although the only clue to her age is that she is a first-time buyer; perhaps an attempt to make the client feel naïve for suggesting buying in Pilton, thus undermining her confidence in her ability to make an astute house purchase. The 'problem' of the client's age is then used to create concerns about their personal safety: "I wouldn't recommend any young female to be there."

When the client suggests taking a look at the estate herself, she is told that she "wouldn't want to", a piece of advice designed to prevent her from even venturing onto the estate. As well as such indirect allusions to potential safety issues, the agent also has more direct ways of provoking fear, alleging that the estate's residents are "drug users et cetera". The agent suggests alternative areas to their client that "are not as close to the Western as you'd like to be", and also betrays a lack of knowledge of the estate, particularly since the regeneration process began. For example, the claim that "There are a lot of high-rise flats" on the estate is not accurate. The built-form on the estate is predominantly walk-up flats, although a large complex of deck-access flats used to dominate part of the estate.

This discussion of estate agents provides strong evidence of the substantial roles they may play in shaping estate images as gatekeepers to owner-occupation. Their attitudes are clearly conditioned by reputations. Many were out of date in their knowledge of the estates and, with the exception perhaps of North Shields, were unaware of the full range of housing opportunities on the estates. Some revealed that they had not visited the estate ever, or for some time. While estate agents are likely to be motivated by a concern to protect their own character as trustworthy businesses and their customers from an 'imprudent' choice, their actions still may undermine regeneration efforts.

Chapter 6 has some practical ideas of how regeneration initiatives can try to make allies of estate agents, given their capacity to undermine change. These ideas build on the observation that in many ways the behaviour of estate agents might actually be against their own interests. For example, in the Edinburgh case in particular, the property market is extremely tight and house prices are generally climbing. In attempting to dissuade prospective clients from considering estates like Pilton, agents are perhaps suppressing the market for such properties and, therefore, their own profits. More generally, new and improved housing developments on previously difficult estates represent an expanding market for owner-occupation and the activities of estate agents, and it could be in their interests to challenge rather than reinforce negative perceptions.

Retail services

Many disadvantaged estates are blighted by poor quality shopping, and often lack a decent supermarket. The nature and quality of retail services provided in an estate affects the quality of life for estate residents, and can also contribute significantly to image building. The quality of shopping sends strong signals to residents about the viability of the local community (or others' perceptions of its viability). For those who are able to move away, disinvestment in local shopping can undermine their confidence in the area. The quality of retail provision is also important in sending signals to outsiders about the future of the estate. Thus retailers usually contribute to the image of an estate by 'responding to' or 'shaping' images.

However, in Castle Vale, Sainsbury's has been persuaded to locate in the shopping centre on the edge of the estate. This business was selected by the HAT partly in order to challenge perceptions of the estate. Potential incomers and local businesses were impressed by the development:

> "It has really made people sit up.... That's mainly because of Sainsbury's profile and the market that they are aiming at you wouldn't traditionally associate with the Castle Vale estate ... I think it does say something about their view of the area as a whole ... that perhaps it has a greater potential than I thought it had." (Employer, Birmingham)

The Sainsbury's development clearly has the potential to help to improve Castle Vale's reputation simply by its presence. In addition, outsiders using the supermarket will be able to witness first hand many of the physical changes on the estate, which again may cause them to re-evaluate their opinion. However, this kind of approach also needs to take account of residents' needs and priorities. For example, some considered Sainsbury's as an expensive shopping option, out of the reach of most residents.

Private housing developers

Private housing developers contribute to building estate images in a similar way to prestigious retailers. Their presence or absence is important for shaping images positively or negatively. Indeed their presence can challenge a poor reputation. This is because they are believed to be sensitive to risk, and their investment decisions are therefore read as an estimate of risk.

The three estates each have new private sector housing developments. The willingness of developers to build on the estates was often perceived as a signal that the estates were improving, especially by budding incomers. Below, one such incomer is looking at a brochure for a new Barratt development on Meadow Well:

> "It makes you think – something good's coming in the future really. When they're building houses, nice houses, they're gonna build facilities for the people living in the houses, so the whole area's gonna change isn't it?" (Potential incomer, Meadow Well)

Employers and estate images

Local employers have an important role to play in the regeneration process. Their locational and recruitment decisions can influence the economic trajectory of the locality and will affect employment opportunities for estate residents. However, employers also have an important function in image building. As Table 5 shows, they respond to and shape images, but are yet to become truly active in challenging images.

Recruiting estate residents

A key way in which employers react to images is in their recruitment practices, particularly in the extent to which they are prepared to recruit from stigmatised estates. Chapter 3 described how estate residents believed that postcode discrimination was practised by employers and that their job opportunities were curtailed through prejudice.

Employers in North Shields, north-west Edinburgh and north-east Birmingham were interviewed for the study. They were asked about postcode discrimination; whether they practised it or thought others did. While all denied that they discriminated many thought others might. Some employers had lower expectations of estate residents in terms of their educational levels and attitudes to work. Others were defensive when denying discrimination. Overall, it was clear that employers were alive to the issue and, aware that discrimination could not be admitted to, gave some hints that it was practised.

Employers were more predisposed to employing estate residents where they already did so. Interestingly, the fact that the estate was undergoing a major regeneration effort could also be a positive influence:

> "The way that the high rise flats have been tackled, the background noise that something is happening has a positive feel good factor.... In your mind you think well perhaps things are making a turn for the better. We will therefore consider people more seriously." (Employer, Birmingham)

Employers are clearly 'responding to' images in terms of their recruitment practices. Chapter 5 examines how the regeneration initiatives are trying to involve employers in the challenging images process, while Chapter 6 has some additional suggestions on how to make stakeholders of employers.

The media and estate images

Chapter 3 discussed how estate residents experience the media as a stigmatising force that labels the estate and its people as problematic. Crucially, newspapers, television and radio not only label but also communicate this label to a wide audience. Table 5 suggested that the main activity of the commercial media in relation to image building is 'shaping images'. This is because their perceptions are available to be consumed by the wider public. The parallel with estate agents is strong.

Interviews with journalists, however, revealed that most believed that they did not shape the news or an estate's image, but simply reacted to it.

Clearly, *how* they react to a problematic reputation will influence the kinds of stories they look for in, and expect to tell about, a place. For example, there is an obvious reliance on negative adjectives. Qualifications such as *sprawling, notorious, problem, run-down* and *vast* are frequently used in the local press to convey complex negative messages about the estates. They are used even where the article is reporting positive news about falls in unemployment or crime. For example:

> "The once notorious Meadow Well estate is now one of the quietest crime free areas in North Tyneside, police have revealed." ('North Shields News', *The Guardian*, 30 October 1997)

Journalists also have the capacity to influence positive perceptions of places. Most suggested that they would be willing to write good news stories about the estates, and there were many examples of coverage of regeneration efforts. However, it is evident that there can be difficulties in reporting regeneration stories. In the same way as the language of reporting often does not suit the estate's residents and regeneration bodies, the language of regeneration is often technical and inaccessible to journalists and their readers. Further, positive regeneration stories are often complex:

> "It's much easier and much more exciting for a journalist to write about joyriders or junkies than it is to write about the problems that single parents have in getting off welfare into work.... That's complicated and not nearly as sexy as 'joyriders kill child'." (Journalist, Edinburgh)

It is clearly not a simple matter to bring journalists on board as allies in challenging images. But, it may be possible to persuade individual journalists that they could tell more good news about an estate than they do. In the next chapter, the attempts of the regeneration initiatives to manage the media are discussed and there are further suggestions for action in Chapter 6.

Conclusion

This chapter has identified the links between a range of actors and how can they affect the sustainability of regeneration on stigmatised estates. It has shown that few private sector organisations contribute positively to the image of stigmatised estates, and indeed, has highlighted how the activities of some can actually undermine the regeneration effort. Chapter 5 explores the role of public sector agencies in the same way. However, a key message emerging from the study is the need to turn actors into stakeholders in the estate's image. Chapter 6 provides some initial suggestions for how such a task could be initiated.

The image managers

Introduction

This chapter explores the issue of who should be responsible for coordinating the task of challenging images of stigmatised estates. It begins by examining the role of selected public-sector service providers in image building, using the framework established in Chapter 4. It argues that although many public agencies participate in regeneration partnerships, perhaps through formal representation on boards or through specific projects, their potential contribution to challenging images is not being maximised.

The chapter then considers the activities of regeneration initiatives in relation to building images. It highlights their potential role in integrating public agencies and private organisations into an overall process capable of tackling an estate's problem reputation. This process can be thought of as 'image management'; that is, a range of activities concerned with promoting positive and minimising negative images, including marketing the estate, media management, and a strategic approach to ensuring that various aspects of the regeneration programme, such as housing improvements or tackling crime, contribute to challenging images.

Public services and estate images

Estate schools

Schools appear to play an important role in all dimensions of image building. Table 5 suggested that local schools were involved in reacting to, shaping and challenging images.

Some residents believed teachers would sometimes react to an estate's reputation by expecting less of pupils:

> "One of my friends, her wee boy wasn't doing very well and the teacher said, 'Oh don't worry, we don't expect them to be geniuses in this school anyway'."
> (Committed resident, Pilton)

The study did not investigate whether such concerns are valid. However, a Head Teacher from one school did confirm that they sometimes discovered this attitude among some teaching staff. Whatever the scale of the problem, this is clearly an example of where schools and teachers can be seen to react to the problem reputation of an estate in a way which can only reinforce rather than challenge stigma.

The capacity for schools to unconsciously shape both positive and negative perceptions of areas emerged strongly from the focus groups. Indeed 'shaping images' appears to be the main role that schools currently perform in relation to image building. Non-residents frequently mentioned the quality of local schools as an important aspect of what makes residential areas attractive. Their decisions about where to live were often strongly affected by the nature of local schools. Individuals would not just avoid particular estates for this reason, but areas that might place them within the catchment area:

> "We had a horrendous time with parents when children were placed here five years ago. Parents threatened to burn themselves to death rather than send their child here. Protest groups ... you name it, that extreme." (Head Teacher)

However, good schools were not simply valued for themselves. For some, the reputation of a school acted as a barometer of what an area was like and could shape perceptions of the estate. Some participants suggested that school league tables could be used in this way. Similarly, knowledge of an area (or its reputation) was also seen as a good indicator of what the school would be like:

> "You only have to look at the kids that are brought up around there, to know what the school's like." (Improbable incomer, Castle Vale)

Because attitudes towards schools and their localities are so closely associated, local schools can also contribute significantly to challenging an estate's image. If outsiders value good schools, then an improving school can give a positive message about an estate and ultimately help to attract new young residents. Indeed, the future trajectory of stigmatised estates and schools located there are clearly intertwined:

> "It's about a change of image of the estate. We would have had to [change the school] regardless but it would have been much harder if hadn't been for the visible changes on the estate that people can see.... It might not have been a possible job without that.... Both of us have helped each other. People see the physical changes, but they could say, 'you're just moving the problem'. But because the school's changing, people see that the estate is on the up." (Head Teacher)

Social landlords

Housing organisations, such as local authority landlords and housing associations are also influential in shaping perceptions of estates. Chapter 4 argued that *private* housing developers could shape images of an estate; their presence was regarded as a sign that the estate was on an upward trajectory, their absence that it was not.

The presence or absence of housing associations can work in a similar way. Despite well-documented problems on English housing association estates, many focus group participants saw the presence of a housing association as a sign of estate improvement. Chapter 2 revealed

the strong views held by some residents and non-residents on the contribution of anti-social behaviour and poor parental control of children, for example, to giving an estate a poor reputation. Such 'people management' issues are often seen as the remit of landlords through effective housing management. Housing associations are believed to have higher standards of housing management and to be less tolerant of anti-social behaviour than local authority landlords. Perceptions of housing management practices were influential in shaping perceptions of estates.

Housing organisations can also influence perceptions of estates through the decisions about the built environment. For example, the early demolition of problematic tower blocks in Castle Vale and deck-access blocks in Pilton sent a clear message about the prospect of change on the estates. Changes to the built form have symbolic importance:

> "I think the loss of the tower blocks was aesthetically a great improvement. I think you still had that perception of tower blocks and, you know, social deprivation.... From our offices all the tower blocks ... have gone and they've been replaced by quite nice, low level flats and it does look much better and it seems to give the impression of being a much nicer estate just from removing those." (Employer, Birmingham)

However, those involved in housing change need to make sure that the design of new developments does not reinforce negative images of estates or their residents. For example hard landscaping may offer increased security but can be interpreted in a negative way:

> "It looks like a prison. There's all these railings. Its looks like they're all behind bars. All these horrible spiky railings." (Improbable incomer, Meadow Well)

The police service

The police are another key public service that could make more of a contribution to challenging estate images. There are some initial signs that, in at least two of the case study estates, the police recognise such a role. But, as Table 5 suggests, police mainly respond to pre-existing images. Chapter 3 documented residents' perceptions that they receive a reduced policing service because of the reputation of their estates.

Physical design issues were also important in relation to policing. The design of the local police station was read as a sign of the police's attitude towards the people on an estate. In Castle Vale, for example, the station has prominent security features, interpreted by some residents as confrontational:

> "It's not a police station is it?... It's got a 20-foot fence round it, to keep them in or to keep us out, we can't work out which." (Probable leaver, Castle Vale)

Police officers recognise that such fortifications can divide the police from the community it serves:

> "What didn't help was when we had the police station which had this large fence around it. And of course a lot of people then made an issue of this ... to some people it gives it a 'them and us' but that clearly isn't the case." (Police Officer)

In contrast the Meadow Well police station is in an almost derelict tower block in waste land on the edge of the estate. The building is not marked as a police station and is unattractive. The impression conveyed by the building is that the service does not take policing on Meadow Well seriously (yet frontline services were largely valued by residents). There are plans to relocate to a more suitable building.

These examples of the designs of police stations have the capacity to shape perceptions of an area and its people for residents and visitors alike. The design of the Castle Vale station, in particular, demands the question: what kind of a place is this if it requires such a well-protected police station?

Interestingly, focus group participants regarded the police as trustworthy sources of information about the character of residential areas. As Chapter 2 showed, crime was a key concern for focus group participants. Budding incomers often wanted assurances about crime rates, and were prepared to believe the police. This suggests that the police may have a key role to play in challenging images and, again, that their input should be maximised.

The police and social landlords contribute to building images both through their response to social problems, such as crime and anti-social behaviour, and through their approach to physical and design issues. Perceptions of how social problems are being tackled are of undoubted importance in challenging images. Often, however, such problems are complex and difficult to solve. Physical design issues are possibly even more important indicators of how desirable an area is, yet may be easier to deal with. For example, high security design, which incorporates railings, shutters and prominent security cameras, is an effective way of conveying that social problems have not yet been resolved. Clearly there is a need to achieve a balance between necessary levels of security and concerns about the interpretation of security measures.

Chapter 4 argued that challenging images will depend on making private-sector service providers allies in the image management process. Based on this discussion of a limited range of public agencies, it is clear that they should also be recruited to the task. The question is, who should be responsible for recruiting these actors, who should the image manager be? Currently regeneration initiatives alone are in a position to take on the task.

Regeneration initiatives and estate images

As detailed in Appendix B each estate currently has a major investment programme underway. They were selected as case studies partly because their initiatives had prioritised addressing the estate's problem reputation and because each was taking a different approach. Table 6 details the approaches to image management taken by the three initiatives.

The study was not designed to evaluate the appropriateness of the approaches taken to image management by the initiatives. However, it is important to explore how different aspects of their approaches have the potential to tackle problem images.

Each initiative has a distinctive philosophy underpinning how it approaches challenging the estate's reputation. The HAT, for example, has emphasised its own profile and the success of the regeneration initiative. However, it recognises that

Table 6: Approaches to image management: the case-study initiatives

	North Edinburgh Area Renewal (Pilton)	Castle Vale Housing Action Trust	Meadow Well SRB

Image-related objectives	• To raise the profile of regeneration internally and externally
	• To challenge the unpopular image of the area
		• Cross-cutting issue within an holistic approach to regeneration
		• Focus on:
		  ○ raising the profile of the HAT
		  ○ addressing stigmatisation
			• First objective of predecessor Estate Action initiative: "to remove stigma attached to the estate"

Strategic/ non-strategic	• Strategic approach • Communications Strategy published 1998	• Programme of planned activities rather than a strategy • PR and communications strategy being developed in 2000	• Largely non-strategic • Activities as necessary
Staffing	• Dedicated part-time PR officer since early 1999 • Previously used PR resources of partners on an occasional basis	• Full-time PR officer and full-time assistant since 1998	• No dedicated staff; use Communications Unit of Council as necessary
Resources	• £18,000 per annum for staffing	• £100,000 per annum for staffing and other activities	• No dedicated resources
Organisational arrangements	• Communications Group established as sub-group of partnership; involves representatives of key partners including community and private sector	• Publicity sub-group for first year • Currently no separate structure, PR officer sits on Management Group to facilitate cross-cutting approach	• No separate part of the structure
Target audiences	• Estate residents • External opinion formers: media, employers, politicians	• Government, regeneration practitioners • External opinion formers: employers, academics • Estate residents	• Local, and occasionally national, media • Estate residents

Key messages	• Progress of regeneration
	• Positive stories of change
	• Specific messages:
	  ○ dynamic changing area
	  ○ history of community involvement
	  ○ diverse area (eg ethnicity, economics)
		• Identity and profile of HAT
		• Positive stories of change
		• Estate facilities - leisure, shopping, arts
		• Progress of regeneration and improving quality of life
			• Positive stories of change
			• Progress of regeneration

Main activities	• Communication with residents, eg through page in local newspaper, leaflets and so on • Media monitoring • Attracting positive media • Media training for community representatives • Re-launch of Business Support Group • Plans for tours of area	• High-profile visitors: the Queen, government ministers • Media monitoring • Attracting positive media • Business Support Group • Sports and arts activities to draw in visitors • Web page, community radio • Newsletter to residents • Customer care	• Attracting positive media attention and challenging negative coverage • Communication with residents, eg newsletter, street meetings

this approach can be double-edged by taking Castle Vale's problems onto the national, and even international stage. Latterly, there has been more of a focus on communicating with estate residents and building and maintaining their trust in the regeneration process. By contrast, NEAR has had a focus on 'communication' from the outset, attempting to ensure good communication about the regeneration process with residents and also regeneration partners. It has deliberately avoided using logos and publicity materials associated with promotional campaigns. The SRB in Meadow Well similarly concentrates on communication rather than publicity, focusing on communicating with residents and with wider audiences through the media.

There are also contrasts between the initiatives in terms of the scale of resources devoted to image issues, and whether dedicated staff have been employed. The HAT is the best resourced of the three initiatives, and has also devoted the most resources and staff time to image management. Thus a budget of around £100,000 per annum is available to cover the costs of two full time staff – a PR officer and assistant – leaving a small budget for specific activities. Consequently, the HAT has been able to develop a sustained programme of promotional activities designed to raise the profile of the HAT and the regeneration process, coupled with cultural and sporting events intended to attract both local people and local press coverage.

Neither NEAR nor the Meadow Well SRB are as well funded as the HAT and their funding of an image management process has also been less well resourced. Both used to rely on specialist PR staff from partner organisations to undertake specific projects, rather than dedicated staff, but since early 1999 NEAR has employed a part-time PR officer. The NEAR PR officer has been able to take a more strategic approach to developing relations with the media and communicating with residents, whereas in Meadow Well the process remains *ad hoc*. There are always competing demands on the resources available to regeneration partnerships. However, if initiatives are to take image management seriously, resources need to be devoted to the task, not least to signal the importance of the issue. Employing dedicated staff may also be important for raising the profile of image issues within the work of the initiative, and may help in the development of a strategic approach.

Chapter 2 revealed that each estate did not have a single image, but was viewed in different ways by distinctive groups of residents and non-residents. It also highlighted how different groups within the young, employed population have different attitudes on why neighbourhoods have problems, as well as distinctive priorities in relation to their own housing needs. Interestingly, none of the three initiatives has yet developed marketing campaigns based on research into the priorities and attitudes of different audiences. NEAR is alone in terms of having identified some specific messages which it wants to communicate about the estate – such as the diversity of the area and its history of community involvement – but even here there has been a tendency to assume that unified positive messages will suffice for all, and attempts to tailor messages to specific audiences have not been undertaken. Some suggestions as to how regeneration initiatives might develop tailored marketing strategies are provided in Chapter 6.

The HAT is the only one of the three initiatives to prioritise attracting non-residents onto the estates as part of an image management strategy. It has done this mainly through developing sporting and arts activities, although it also sought to entice a large supermarket onto the estates, which will bring outsiders to the estate's boundaries. Drawing non-residents onto an estate to witness changes for themselves seems to be an essential part of the image management process. The potential incomers who participated in the focus groups fell into three main groups:

1. Never visit the estates, or had not visited since regeneration began (may drive past but don't visit).
2. Visit sporadically over time.
3. Visit on a more regular basis (for example to use the swimming baths, visit a friend).

The third group seem much more likely to consider moving to the estates, and often took pains to educate less knowledgeable members of groups about the extent of change, with a focus on the visible signs of regeneration.

One potential incomer to Pilton contrasted the estate with another Edinburgh estate undergoing regeneration, Wester Hailes, in terms of its capacity to draw them to it:

> "I mean, it's not like you can say, oh there's a good shopping centre there

[Pilton] or, I don't know, a DIY warehouse or something. There's actually nothing there. There's no reason to go. I mean I'm out at Wester Hailes now more than I ever was because of the Westside Plaza, the cinema complex out there. There's nothing like that. I mean, I would never have dreamed of going out to Wester Hailes before in my life but I'm out there quite a lot now at the pictures." (Doubtful incomer, Pilton)

However, developing new facilities to attract outsiders in can backfire unless the facilities are made available only when the regeneration process is well underway. This problem can again be illustrated in relation to the Wester Hailes estate. Despite massive investment there, including significant housing change as well as the development of state of the art facilities, one participant still saw some incongruity:

"It's a lovely cinema and you go to that and that's fine, but you walk into it, there's five security guards checking the car park for you. You look at the high-rise around it and the police are always in two's – and its actually two cars – and this kind of thing makes you go, 'I don't want to live here'." (Doubtful incomer, Pilton)

Turning saboteurs into stakeholders

The remainder of this chapter explores the ways in which the three initiatives have attempted to engage with some of the actors involved in image building. Specifically, it examines the extent to which the initiatives have taken deliberate steps to turn private sector and public sector interests into stakeholders in the process of challenging images of the estate.

The initiatives have each attempted to engage with some private sector actors. They have sought to involve local employers in the regeneration task, and both private housing developers and the retail sector have been targeted for their potential contribution to the regeneration programme. Both the Castle Vale HAT and NEAR in Pilton have sought to entice a high street bank to locate on the estate. However, none of the initiatives has specifically tried to bring representatives from the house selling industry (eg estate agents and property surveyors) on board, nor other financial institutions such as insurance companies or credit

agencies. Further, while the initiatives have sought to connect employers, retailers and housing developers to the regeneration task, this has tended to be for other purposes rather than image management. This distinction can be illustrated in relation to employers.

Regeneration initiatives generally have a reasonable track record of engaging with local businesses and employers, usually through the mechanism of Business Support Groups (BSGs). The rationale for doing this is generally to enlist their support in the difficult task of economic regeneration. A variety of mechanisms exist to make employer involvement a reality, many of which are geared towards maximising economic benefits from engaging employers. Additional or complementary benefits of employer involvement, such as those that can contribute to challenging images, are not always recognised.

However, in both Castle Vale and Pilton employers are recruited to BSGs partly to challenge their image of the estate:

"The Castle Vale Business Group is an example of a way by which you target that particular group ... you're trying to get them to take you seriously and say 'well these are people like anybody else. Why stigmatise them just because they've got B35 [post code]'." (HAT employee, Castle Vale)

Challenging the attitude of employers towards estates and their residents is a vital first step in turning potential image saboteurs into stakeholders in the image management process. However, there is also recognition that more is at stake than changing the attitudes and practices of just those employers involved in a BSG. Employers are seen as important opinion formers who have the potential to influence the perceptions of the estate among a wider influential audience.

Thus, there has been some attempt to draw private-sector agencies into the regeneration process, although so far only employers have been targeted specifically as part of an image management strategy. This contrasts with a lack of attention to the role that public-sector agencies could be persuaded to play. Although, public-sector agencies sit on the boards of partnerships and contribute to the regeneration process in general, they do not tend to be involved specifically in the task of image management. As highlighted earlier, the activities of agencies such as police, schools and landlords can contribute to sustaining as well as challenging images. However, where their contribution is positive it is more likely to be a consequence of luck than design. Chapter 6 makes some suggestions for how regeneration initiatives can move towards engaging public-sector services in the image task and makes further suggestions on how to involve private sector organisations.

Managing the media

Finally, media management is an arena where all three initiatives have been energetic, having recognised the critical role played by the local press in particular in shaping perceptions of the estate. Both NEAR and the Castle Vale HAT have adopted similar approaches to the media. The nature of media coverage is monitored to ascertain whether it presents the estate and the regeneration process in a positive or negative light, and changes in the balance of coverage are seen as an index of whether the initiative is being successful in challenging the estate's problem reputation. Both initiatives also place an emphasis on securing positive media coverage; the responsibilities of their PR officers include writing press releases telling 'good news' stories about the estates and developing effective working relationships with journalists. In both, relationship building is regarded as an ongoing, incremental process.

Both initiatives report increased positive press coverage of the estates and journalists interviewed commented on the usefulness of well-written press releases. Additionally, in Pilton, community activists have undergone media training to help them develop the skills required to become effective advocates for the estates and to understand some of the potential pitfalls of contact with the media. There are plans in Castle Vale to do the same.

In Meadow Well a slightly different approach has been taken. There is less of a focus on monitoring coverage. They concentrate on attracting positive coverage and it is also common for negative coverage to be directly *challenged* by the initiative. Thus while there are attempts to develop constructive relationships with individual journalists, this is matched by a willingness to confront and try to correct negative coverage. The

other initiatives have rejected this approach believing that it may be counter-productive.

All three estates continue to attract media coverage that emphasises current or past problems. However, they have also enjoyed significant positive publicity in recent years, most of which reports the successes of the regeneration effort. However, focus-group participants tended to believe that the balance of coverage was still predominately negative and, unsurprisingly, there was a propensity to remember dramatic stories that dwelled on problems, rather than those which accentuated positive developments. There were also a number of instances where articles believed by initiatives to be positive, were interpreted by participants in a negative light. For example, a story about a healthy eating initiative in Pilton was seen as patronising by residents, reinforcing perceptions that they did not know how to look after themselves or their families adequately.

Conclusion

This chapter has explored how the regeneration initiatives have approached the problem of image, noting how the issue has been prioritised, resourced and approached within the context of the wider regeneration agenda. It suggests that although the initiatives are taking the issue seriously, there are significant gaps in their approaches. Image management implies a need to take account of the full range of factors that influence neighbourhoods and how they are perceived. In making an assessment of an area, residents and potential residents do not discriminate between those aspects of an estate that are being tackled directly by regeneration projects and those that are not. Their evaluation of the amenity of an area will depend on their judgement of, for example, the quality of schooling, cleansing and housing management services, the cost of home insurance and their perception of riskiness of the neighbourhood in terms of crime, property values and effect on their own and children's opportunities. Importantly, public-sector agencies are not routinely operating as stakeholders in the process of challenging images of the estates, and only a few private-sector organisations are involved. The next chapter provides some suggestions as to how image management might be more appropriately organised at the neighbourhood level, as well as further ideas on how to engage with public and private-sector agencies.

6

Challenging images: suggestions for action

This chapter offers practical suggestions for how a problem reputation can be tackled as part of a regeneration initiative. It addresses different dimensions of the problem. First, it discusses who the 'image manager' should be, discussing organisational arrangements as well as the skills required. It then suggests ways image managers can include a range of actors in the processes of challenging images. The third section returns to the concerns of Chapters 2 and 3 and considers ways in which image managers can connect with residents and potential residents and the final section suggests some modifications to regeneration practice.

This chapter should not be read as a recipe for success, or even a set of good practice guidelines. Image management in the context of stigmatised estates is still too recent a phenomenon to allow the main ingredients of a successful strategy to be identified with confidence. However, the chapter draws on the experience gained by the three initiatives, contextualised within a broader understanding of marketing, and provides initial suggestions as how this difficult problem could begin to be tackled.

Organising image management

The evidence of this study is that organisational issues are important for effective image management. That perceptions of an estate are influenced by the activities of a wide range of actors is critical. Yet, the study has found that few of these actors contribute substantially to challenging images. This suggests the need for organisational arrangements that draw them into image management.

In each estate, the regeneration process is marshalled by an initiative involving a range of public-sector players alongside representatives from the private and community sectors. Despite this, none of the three has effectively engaged the full range of actors in image management, and some actors continue to sustain rather than challenge stigma. The problem may lie in the fact that regeneration initiatives are not usually seen as *the* central point of authority within a neighbourhood for all public agencies. Further, they rely on the voluntary participation of private-sector organisations. What is needed is an individual or structure that has both authority over public-sector agencies and capacity to influence the private sector. In other words, an 'image manager' of significant stature is required.

The image manager could potentially be the manager of the regeneration initiative. However, recent proposals by the government's Social Exclusion Unit (SEU) to pilot 'neighbourhood management' (see Taylor, 1999) appear to offer some important refinements to current regeneration practice that might also provide an effective vehicle for image management. The SEU's proposals include having someone 'in charge' at neighbourhood level, as well as using appropriately decentralised and reorganised mainstream public services as the key instrument of renewal. Both proposals would also be useful to image management. A neighbourhood manager to whom public sector agencies were accountable could build awareness of the need for an holistic approach to challenging images.

The findings of the study also suggest that skills and technical expertise are important to image management. However, it is not clear that all of the necessary expertise is available to regeneration initiatives as they are currently organised. Two case-study initiatives employed public relations staff, although this is unlikely to be necessary or affordable for all regeneration projects.

The skills needed by an effective image manager (or neighbourhood manager) are, arguably, mainly those skills currently required by regeneration managers:

- networking skills and the ability to facilitate joint working;

- sufficient seniority, authority and 'people skills' to exert the influence required for the above task;

- experience in more than one sector, or a well-developed sense of empathy, in order to have credibility with the full range of actors;

- a sophisticated understanding of the regeneration process;

- refined communication skills, effective in a wide range of sectors and with people from a variety of backgrounds.

However, image managers may also require competencies not traditionally associated with neighbourhood work. These might include:

- an understanding of marketing;

- experience of working with the media;

- an understanding of the processes and pitfalls of promotional activity and public relations.

Importantly, image managers will not need to be specialists in any or all of these fields, but they will need sufficient understanding of them to enable them to guide specialist staff in their remit of challenging images.

Of course, effective image management will not occur simply as a result of improved organisational arrangements. Image managers need to have the right kinds of tools and strategies at their disposal that will allow them to successfully market the estate. The study has identified two distinctive groupings of people whose perceptions need to be influenced in order for stigma to be challenged. The first, discussed earlier, involves the private- and public-sector actors who need to be recruited as stakeholders in the image management process. The second involves residents and potential residents of the estates who need to be convinced that the estate is improving. Strategies for influencing each are suggested in the following sections of the chapter.

Encouraging the stakeholders

Changes on the estates need to be marketed to private- and public-sector actors in order to persuade them to change their attitude and behaviour towards the estates. There is a need to increase the stock of private-sector actors involved in the regeneration process generally and, in so doing, help them to develop a stake in improving the estates' reputations. In relation to public-sector actors, perhaps the key issue is to raise their awareness of how they can contribute to challenging images.

Arguably there are two main strategies open to image managers here:

- First, a few actors may be brought on board by alerting them to the damage they are causing to the regeneration process and the lives of residents. Thus, it may be possible to persuade them to adjust their behaviour by educating them about the impoverishing and discriminating effects that stigma creates. This might be considered the *altruistic* strategy.

- Second, image managers could recruit allies by making it in the interests of the individuals or their organisations to help. Marketing is based on the premise that people are motivated to act where they see benefit to themselves. So actors would be helped to recognise how challenging the image of an estate may help them do their own job more effectively, or be a source of profit for them. This can be thought of as the *self-interest* strategy.

The following discussion considers how to make stakeholders of private-sector businesses, public-sector services and the media. It argues that the self-interest strategy is likely to be the most effective, but that image managers could also usefully communicate with actors about the destructive impacts of stigma.

Make allies of the private sector

Image managers need to find ways of engaging private-sector organisations in ways which help them do their jobs more effectively, and which help them to recognise how they might benefit from an improved estate image.

Selling the estate to estate agents, insurance companies and so on

The report has revealed the damage that estate agents, insurance companies, property surveyors and so on can cause to an estate's image. Their capacity to sabotage or undermine regeneration efforts has been evidenced in a number of ways. Image managers need to find ways of involving such agencies that simultaneously challenge their negative perceptions of the estates but also help them in their own tasks.

One idea worth pursuing is to bring estate agents onto the estates so that they can update their knowledge of environmental changes, improvements to local facilities and housing developments. Such visits would have the aim of marketing the estate to the agent as a place of residential choice, so may have to be carefully managed. Visits could then be followed up with mailings advising of further developments. The impact of the initiative could be monitored by replicating our mystery shopper survey, although there is the danger of antagonising agents and losing their goodwill.

Crucially, however, selling the estate to estate agents is not likely to rely on obtaining goodwill. Rather it will depend on their recognising an opportunity to increase the saleability of hitherto 'difficult to sell' properties on their books, and perhaps the opportunity to allow property prices on these estates to rise in parallel with prices elsewhere in the local housing market. This strategy is likely to work best in particular housing market contexts. For example, in Edinburgh the property market is very tight, and there may well be latent demand for estates such as Pilton. However, this is less likely to be the case in the North East of England.

A similar approach might apply to insurance companies. Where crime rates are falling on estates, it would be worth alerting insurance companies to the fact. It may also be possible to influence their assessment of risk by bringing them onto the estate to witness improved security and design changes. An additional strategy might be to work intensively with a selected number of companies to show them that the estates may offer a new market for their business. The study has confirmed that residents of stigmatised estates can find insurance difficult to obtain or premiums prohibitive. A company that offers new opportunities or undercuts other insurers may generate enough business to cover its risk.

Getting employers on board

The three initiatives studied are all involved in enlisting employer support for the regeneration process, with recent attempts in both Castle Vale and Pilton to re-energise Business Support Groups (BSGs). Involvement in such groups is often sold to business as a form of enlightened self-interest; thus the business itself will gain through helping to facilitate improvements to an estate or to the lives of residents, normally through increasing the economic opportunities available to residents. Clearly such groups can also be useful mechanisms for challenging the negative perceptions may hold about the estate. Through their involvement some employers may even be encouraged to act as advocates for the estate, spreading the story of renewal within their networks.

However, interviews with employers suggested that they do not have a detailed understanding of the regeneration process, even if involved in BSGs. Overall, there was a tendency to know about regeneration simply through observing visible works, and for there to be a lack of knowledge of the breadth of the regeneration agenda. A few employers will gladly take part in committees such as BSGs but this is a relatively demanding role and many will not participate. However, this latter group were keen to know what was going on the estate.

Publicity materials about the regeneration process in the three estates were shown to employers. Reactions to this material were generally positive and suggested the potential for simple literature to affect the views of this group. Thus a complementary strategy to BSGs is to distribute information that keeps employers up to date with developments on the estate. Most had never received such information, yet thought they would read leaflets about the regeneration process, provided they were clearly written; as in the response to one below:

> "Great, I mean I wouldn't have realised that it was such a massive task. Here it says it's the largest postwar municipal

estate. So how many people live on the Vale? Well that's a start isn't it.... Yes this makes me feel much more comfortable. Personally I think they should be shouting this kind of stuff from the roof."
(Employer, Birmingham)

Employers are an important target group for image managers, not least because their recruitment decisions have a direct impact on the lives of residents, and therefore on the economic profile of the estate. However, their importance also lies in their links to other business people. Securing them as advocates of the estates, or at least lessening their propensity to act as deliberate or inadvertent detractors, may be critical in securing an estate's economic future.

Recruiting the public sector

Public-sector services must also be co-opted by image managers. Both the *altruistic* and the *self-interest* strategy have the potential to work in these cases. Public-sector agencies need to be alerted to the damage they can cause by not being aware of the 'image effects' of their activities. The duty of care that drives the public sector is likely to influence their susceptibility to change their practices. However, appeals to the self-interest of public-sector organisations and their employees may also be helpful. Clearly, it is in their interests to do their jobs as effectively as possible. Landlords will be keen to maximise demand for properties in the area, and schools to improve their own popularity through 'piggy-backing' on the perceived success of the regeneration process. The challenge for image managers is to help public-sector agencies recognise the common ground between the effectiveness of their core activities and an improved estate image.

Managing the media

Chapter 5 described how the three initiatives prioritised trying to improve press coverage of the estate and had different techniques for managing the media. Two strategies arise from their activities: *nurturing* and *communicating*.

Build relationships with journalists

The nurturing approach is proactive, centred on good personal relationships between image managers, journalists and editors. As one journalist advised:

"Start feeding them stories. And like nine times out of ten – positive stories – loads of times they'll never be used. Sometimes they will be used because newspapers are always desperate to fill their pages. Even if it's just small fillers or anchors. And they're always looking for ideas for features and stuff like that." (Journalist, Edinburgh)

Again, the key to enlisting journalists as stakeholders is to help them to do their jobs more effectively. Giving them a story that no one else has is an important basis of exchange. Additionally, this person-centred approach might kill some negative stories before they get to print:

"If a bad news story's about to break then you can get your side of the story and give a positive spin on it.... You can say look this is about to happen. It's actually a storm in a teacup. It's not a story.... It might never surface." (Journalist, Birmingham)

For example, reporting on school exam results can be managed in ways that help both journalists and stigmatised estates. Even when results are disappointing, image managers can be proactive, offering a positive slant or at least an explanation:

"I don't know of an estate or a school that anticipates those league tables coming out and before they come out contacts the Education Correspondent. They should say 'look, they're coming out tomorrow, we know that it says we're bottom of the league but the reason we're bottom of the league is blah blah blah'." (Journalist, Birmingham)

Building relationships with journalists can be attempted in a number of ways and with different degrees of intensity. Image managers can choose to try to forge close working relationships with a few journalists, although the high turnover in the news desks in many local newspapers may mean that efforts can be wasted. A complementary or alternative strategy is to host regular events aimed at updating a number of journalists about progress on the estate.

Getting the message to journalists

Communicating with journalists, is also an important aspect of image management. There was some frustration from journalists about the nature of press releases issued by initiatives, particularly the language used in them and reliance on formulaic approaches.

Journalists agree that key components of an effective press release are:

- plain language, not regeneration jargon;

- sufficient detail and a 24-hour contact number;

- quotes from key players;

- focus on human interest ordinary people not organisations or VIPs;

- photo opportunities that are happy, quirky and human interest (not cheque presentations);

- incorporation of key statistics or figures (eg expenditure).

Finally, there is a need to recognise the constraints operating on individual journalists. While good relationships can be developed and attention can usefully be paid by initiatives to how they communicate with the media, even sympathetic journalists can find that their efforts to move away from clichéd, negative reporting are undermined when the story is edited:

"'Sprawling housing estate', 'high rise ghetto'.... That is inserted by the news desk once you send your story over, and it's inserted for colour. How you stop newspapers using clichés I've no idea." (Journalist, Edinburgh)

Targeted image management: residents and potential incomers

This section returns to the themes of Chapters 2 and 3 to suggest how image management could be used to help *retain* existing residents and *attract* young, employed people from neighbouring areas.

The target audiences

Chapter 2 demonstrated that different perceptions of the estates are held by different fractions of the resident and non-resident population. Six distinctive groups were identified who distinguished different assets and problems in the estates and had varying expectations for the estate's future. These groups are sufficiently homogenous to form viable audiences for a targeted marketing strategy. However, while the groups were consistent across the three case studies, image managers should not assume that they will occur in all estates, and will need to undertake their own research. Replicating the design of this study may be useful for this.

Figure 6 is a refinement of Figure 5, which illustrated the groups' warmth towards the estates. It illustrates the groups' likely responsiveness to image management, based on their attitudes to the estates and to publicity and promotional material about the estates.

One interpretation of Figure 6 might be that image managers should focus their efforts on those groups towards the top of the thermometer and ignore those nearer the bottom. Further, given that committed residents have already chosen to stay, efforts should perhaps be directed towards persuading budding incomers to move to the estate. While this is broadly accurate, the story is a little more complicated.

Figure 6: Sensitivity to image management: a thermometer

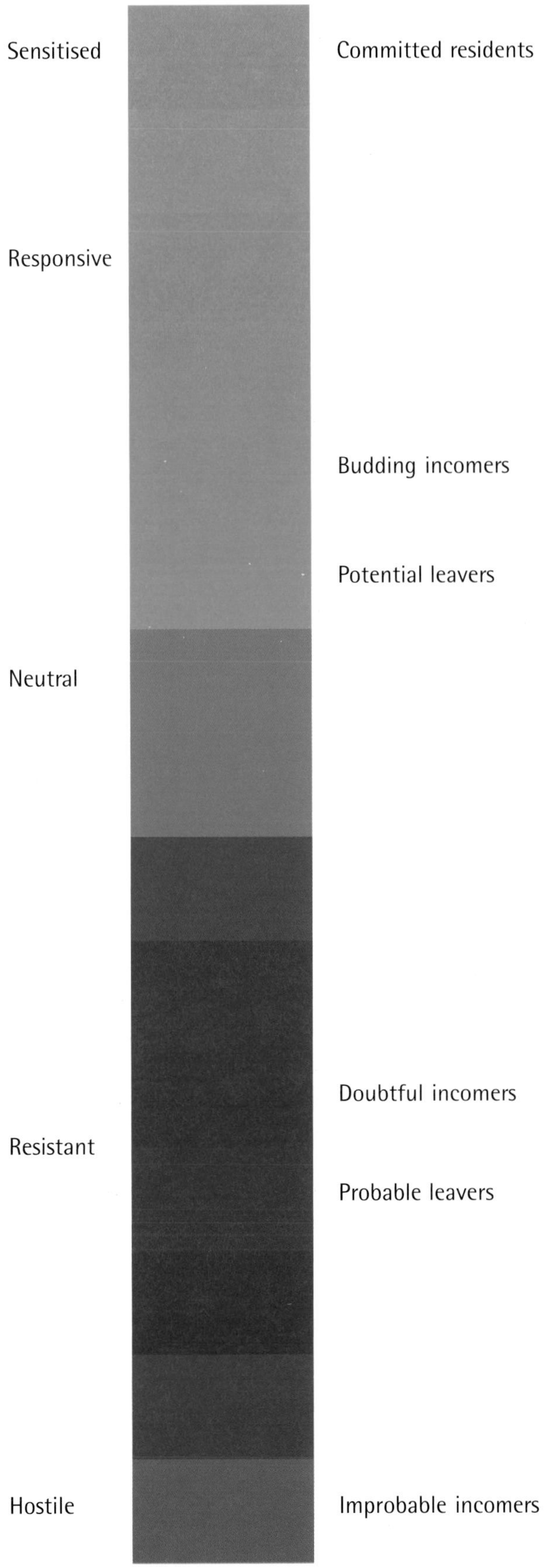

Sensitised	Committed residents
Responsive	
	Budding incomers
	Potential leavers
Neutral	
	Doubtful incomers
Resistant	Probable leavers
Hostile	Improbable incomers

While probable leavers and doubtful incomers are likely to be resistant to attempts to challenge their image of an estate, they will not be completely hostile or dismissive of such efforts. In particular, given that the probable leaver groups included recent incomers to the estates, there are considerable risks involved in developing an image management approach that ignores them. Effective marketing requires customer care: following up and looking after those who respond to promotional strategies. Without this, today's budding incomers may become tomorrow's probable leavers. Further, dissatisfied people tend to tell others about their dissatisfaction. Probable leavers can be an important source of negative images of the estates, which are give credence by other outsiders. We know this from those former residents who have moved away from the estates and attended non-resident focus groups. Thus, a key challenge for a successful marketing strategy would be to find a way of addressing the concerns of this group.

Moving to the top of the thermometer, the committed residents are probably less amenable to persuasion by image strategies than the budding incomers. This is because living on an estate with a problem reputation can *sensitise* residents to images of their estate. For this group, image management can be an extremely important part of the regeneration process; the estate's problem reputation directly impacts on their lives. They are likely, therefore, to value efforts to challenge negative images, and may already be challenging images themselves. However, this sensitivity to the negative images of their estate is also likely to mean a heightened sensitivity to messages. Care will need to be taken not to alienate existing committed residents in the attempt to attract new residents.

Figure 6 should therefore be handled with care. Its usefulness as a tool for identifying target audiences for image management purposes will depend on having a knowledge of the characteristics of the people who make up the six group types, as well as understanding their perceptions of the estate. However, different key target audiences will be responsive to different strategies and even distinctive messages about the estate. Therefore there is a need to be able to distinguish different audiences in order to tailor image strategies to their needs.

Table 7: The varied impact of messages on target groups

Message	Sensitised (Committed residents)	Responsive (Budding incomers)	Neutral (Potential leavers)	Resistant (Probable leavers and doubtful incomers)	Hostile (Improbable incomers)
"There is a master plan for the whole estate"	Important message to nurture and reward commitment	Key message with the potential to encourage risk taking	Could help persuade them to stay – needs timescale for completion of estate attached	Helpful message, particularly for doubtful incomers, but unlikely to overcome resistance on its own	Unlikely to have an effect – could be seen "as throwing good money after bad"
"Local residents are involved in the process of change"	Likely to know about community activities anyway, and may be keen to improve resident input	Key message to encourage confidence both in the sustainability of regeneration and characteristics of potential neighbours	May be cynical about consultation with residents, and will want to see evidence of improvements	Leavers: invitations to join in may help connectedness Incomers: likely to see the estate as lacking community spirit and so possible impact	No impact or incredulity, especially given their hostility to estate residents
"Attempts are being made to challenge the problem reputation"	Key message – stigma affects their lives, something needs to be done	Important message – think the image is probably undeserved, but may still affect willingness to live there	Neutral message, but image is not the main problem	Unimportant – image reflects reality	Waste of effort – image reflects reality
"The reputation is undeserved"	Know this anyway, but appreciate attempts to reinforce it	Important message – may want to see evidence, eg crime statistics	May provoke hostility – "it is deserved on the most part, and I suffer because of it"	Leavers: as for neutrals Incomers: may provoke derision; will need substantial evidence	Will provoke derision
"It's not just a council estate"	Potential to provoke hostility – "What's wrong with being a council tenant?"	Important message – value social mix and see owners as role models	Could be helpful – may be persuaded to stay if given opportunity to buy at below market price, or to rent from a housing association	Leavers: no impact, unlikely to rent again Incomers: may be unaware of tenure mix and could be tempted by discounts	Likely to be new, even interesting information

Message	Sensitised (Committed residents)	Responsive (Budding incomers)	Neutral (Potential leavers)	Resistant (Probable leavers and doubtful incomers)	Hostile (Improbable incomers)
"It's next to so and so desirable area"	May be counter-productive – has potential to undermine pride in estate	Useful message – has the potential to impress people, they think they are getting a bargain	May already claim to live there!	Leavers: "It hasn't made any difference so far" Incomers: unlikely to be impressed	Might stop them moving to the desirable area
"There's effective housing management and strong policing"	Will want to experience improvements	Important message – but danger of being overplayed and backfiring	Will want to experience improvements	Leavers: not their experience Incomers: important message, will want zero-tolerance of crime and anti-social behaviour	"Why should we pay for this from our taxes?"
"It's not the same people who live there"	Will provoke hostility and undermine confidence	May be comforted that 'bad apples' have gone, but may worry about affect on community spirit	Important message – may help persuade them to stay	Important message – possible reconsideration	The only message to carry any weight and will want evidence
"Come and see the difference for yourself"	Strong support – "Talk to me and I'll tell you how nice it is"	Tempting, but will want warts-and-all picture	Not relevant/no reaction	Leavers: not relevant but likely to be incredulous Incomers: likely to be wary, and will need hand-holding	Unlikely to consider it – unless they hear positive reports from other people 'like them'
"The estate's name will be changed"	Could provoke community conflict, may undermine confidence	Important message – part of the package that would tempt them	Neutral – unlikely to make a difference	Leavers: won't make any difference Incomers: is necessary, but not sufficient to tempt me	Mud sticks

Key messages to sell an estate and their likely impact on different target groups

Having identified the target groups for a marketing strategy and their susceptibility to image management, the next stage is to identify the kinds of messages about the estate that will challenge their perceptions. Table 7 identifies some key positive messages that image managers might want to promote. These are the messages that residents and potential incomers want to hear about the estates. Some relate to problems they need to know are being tackled. Others relate to concerns about the regeneration process itself. Others refer to the burgeoning assets of the estates. Table 7 also estimates the likely response to the message of the target groups. It emphasises the need to tailor messages to specific groups.

As can be seen from Table 7, not all target groups are likely to respond positively to the messages. In particular, the groups of improbable incomers are either unaffected by, or will deride, most of the messages. They are unlikely to be impressed by the idea that the estate borders a desirable area, and may dismiss attempts to convey the idea that the estate's poor reputation is undeserved. For this group, the only messages to have any significance for them are those that emphasise the fact that the estate is not single tenure, or that previous residents have left.

Conversely, the very messages that could be helpful in challenging the views of improbable incomers could alienate existing committed residents and potentially undermine local pride and solidarity. Thus, attempts to challenge the image of the estate through messages that some non-residents might find welcome could be counter-productive for sensitised residents. Clearly, image managers need to take great care of an estate's committed residents. There are a number of positive messages that can help to reward their commitment, such as being told that attempts are being made to challenge the estate's poor reputation. There are other messages that will be welcome to them, such as news about improved policing. However, these too could backfire, unless residents actually experience improvements.

Some other features of Table 7 deserve comment. First, the three groups in the middle of the table, the responsive, neutral and resistant groups, are all amenable to persuasion by the right message underpinned by real change. Clearly, budding incomers are much more likely to respond to positive images than are probable leavers, but there is a continuum of persuadability between the groups. Second, it is worth highlighting that the key message for all but the hostile groups, and that carries few dangers of backfiring, is the message that there is an overall plan for the estate. There was strong evidence that residents and incomers alike need to know that regeneration covers a range of issues and also to know that the estate will be finished and that parts will not be left untouched.

Finally, despite the difficulties in persuading improbable incomers to move to the estates, it is important that image managers do not give up on this group entirely. This group represents the colleagues, service providers and chance acquaintances who continue to stigmatise the estates and whose views impoverish the lives of residents. Unless the general background noise of stigma can also be resolved, it will be difficult for these kinds of estates to shake free entirely from their problem reputations. Tackling this issue requires both action at the local level and also at the national, political level. Thus, the effectiveness of neighbourhood initiatives to combat stigma will also depend on moves to dispel the stigma of the social rented sector more generally.

Modifying regeneration practice

A focus on image management has some further implications for more traditional aspects of regeneration practice. Below are some suggestions on how aspects of the regeneration process can be made to contribute to effective image management.

Make regeneration visible

Potential incomers to the estates generally had little appreciation of the scale of change in the estates. This finding applied both to the focus groups with residents living near to the estates, and to employers. Participating in the research provided new, often welcome, information about the nature and extent of regeneration to these groups. This is not to say that the regeneration of the estates was entirely invisible to non-residents. However, they were more aware of the ways in which the estates had been dismantled – such as the demolition of eight dominant high-rise blocks in Castle Vale – than they were of the ways in which the estates were being rebuilt. This is largely because much of the regeneration effort has focused on the interior of the estates, rather than on those parts visible to a passer-by.

These findings have clear implications for the future practice of regeneration. Attention could usefully be paid to:

- early demolition of problematic (and prominent!) high-rise or deck-access blocks sends an important signal that change is on the way. However, for non-residents the importance of this highly visible early action declines, unless they actually witness the process of re-building;
- prioritising physical improvements that are visible to non-residents. Thus, 'corridor regeneration' can have a big impact from an image management perspective. However, committed residents should be *involved* in deciding to focus early action on visible sites and should also be reassured that the interior of the estate will be tackled;
- using billboards and banners at strategic sites to tell non-residents about the scale of change on the estate. Visual images are a powerful way of communicating the scale and complexity of the regeneration effort: for example, aerial photographs showing the estate's interior.

Draw non-residents onto the estates

As well as making change visible to non-residents as they pass by, there is a need to encourage non-residents to actually visit or pass through estates. This might imply changes to road layouts or other infrastructure to reduce the physical isolation of many estates. Developing strategies to attract non-residents is another facet of making change visible and is a key message from this research. But such strategies can carry risks. Expensive, facilities may exclude many residents and create opposition from those who remain in poor housing. Again residents must be involved in deciding on this approach.

Both of these suggestions emphasise the importance of physical renewal to regeneration. Arguably, the current emphasis on countering social exclusion through social and economic

measures has down played the importance of physical measures. However, the evidence of this study is that both are necessary, for regeneration generally, and for image management specifically. Initiatives to make physical regeneration work more effectively for image management should be seen as complementary to the social exclusion agenda.

Look after existing residents

Finally, the need to look after existing residents, in order to retain those who are committed to an estate and stem the flow of disgruntled leavers cannot be overemphasised. Image management must involve customer care, and existing 'customers' must not be alienated. Also crucial is the need to support those budding incomers who do actually move to the estates. The evidence of the research is that new owner-occupiers on the estates can feel isolated in their new homes. Community development with new owners could be a useful way of mitigating this and stopping them from becoming the next generation of leavers.

Conclusion: the need for substantive change

Challenging the problem image of an estate cannot be achieved through positive publicity and promotion alone. Activity designed to challenge the negative images of housing estates must be underpinned by substantial, sustained investment. Economic, physical and social problems must be fundamentally tackled before there is any prospect of success in challenging images. Thus the suggestions and recommendations for action contained in this report apply *only* to estates undergoing fundamental change. We would speculate that attempts to challenge the image problem of an estate in the absence of attempts to address other problems would create anger and hostility from residents and would risk generating incredulity and derision from the outside world.

Image management goes beyond promotion and publicity and implies a strategic approach to the challenging images. It demands awareness of the *image implications* of the full range of activities associated with regeneration, and action both to capitalise on opportunities and to mitigate risks.

Challenging images: implications for policy and practice

The development of effective image management presents a number of challenges for regeneration policy and practice.

Implications for regeneration policy

It's time to take stigma seriously

The existence of neighbourhoods with persistent problem reputations has been recognised for a number of years. For too long, it has been assumed either that these reputations will disappear in the wake of a package of regeneration measures; or conversely that poor image is an intractable problem about which nothing much can be done. The findings of this research suggest that direct measures *must* be taken to address the problem, because:

- stigma blights people's lives. It impoverishes those who live in stigmatised neighbourhoods socially and economically;
- the persistence of stigma is a drag on regeneration. Unless it is tackled, people will continue to move out of stigmatised areas, and new residents will be discouraged from moving in. Employers, estate agents and other key actors will continue to undervalue people or property from such neighbourhoods and the long-term sustainability of the regeneration effort will be in peril.

Something can be done about stigma

Despite the fact that the problem reputations of neighbourhoods have strong historical roots and are difficult to shift, the findings from this study suggest that something *can*, and therefore *should* be done about stigma. The suggestions for action

contained in the report cut across almost the entire regeneration agenda.

Resources and training will be essential

Tackling stigma requires resources including for specialist staffing, for well-researched and evaluated marketing strategies and to support a broad base of neighbourhood activities. Resources may also be required to train non-specialist staff in, for example, marketing or media management and community representatives in media relations.

Implications for regeneration practice

Challenging images must be underpinned by substantial change

Any attempt to tackle a problem reputation through image management and marketing must be founded on real material change on the estates. Substantial programmes designed to tackle key physical, economic and social problems must be underway for an image management strategy to have any credibility. Without such underpinning, image management is likely to provoke anger from residents and derision from outsiders.

The timing and tone of image management should be appropriate

Again image management must be grounded in reality. Some of the actions suggested in Chapter 6 may only be applicable once there are visible developments on the estates. In addition, in the early years of the regeneration process a moderate tone to marketing and promotional activities will be appropriate.

Image management cuts across the entire regeneration agenda

Image management and marketing should not be seen as a discrete activity within the regeneration process. Rather an awareness of 'image implications' should be integral to the full range of activities and programmes undertaken. Crucially, the capacity for image management strategies to improve perceptions of a neighbourhood, requires a focus on the 'whole neighbourhood' that is, on the entire package including quality of services and neighbourhood amenity.

Maximise the stock of stakeholders in challenging images

The full range of agencies, actors and activities that influence the character of the neighbourhood need to be co-opted to the task of challenging images. There is a need to increase the stock of stakeholders who have something to gain from improving the estate's image. Both public and private-sector agencies need to be brought on board through targeted activities.

A stigma audit should be carried out at the outset of an initiative

A baseline audit of perceptions of an estate will be important to gauge the success of image management. A range of indicators could be used including perceptions of residents and non-residents, assessing media coverage and noting the performance of, for example, the estate's schools in attracting pupils. Progress in relation to these indicators will suggest an improving reputation.

Regeneration initiatives need to exploit the potential of marketing

Properly targeted campaigns based on an understanding of the distinctive audiences and their interests will be much more successful than undifferentiated publicity or advertising. Marketing needs to be based on thorough research to understand the nature of the target populations, careful development of campaigns designed to address their priorities, followed up

with accurate evaluation of outcomes. Otherwise, the effectiveness of any strategy cannot be judged.

An holistic approach to marketing is required

Marketing does not simply seek to attract new customers, but involves a range of activities designed to keep the loyalty of pre-existing and new customers. In the context of estate regeneration, this means that marketing must also reward existing residents, including those who are not the main targets of campaigns designed to promote social and economically mixed communities. Customer care should also be integral the strategy. New residents must be cared for. They need to be turned into committed residents rather than allowed to become disappointed probable leavers.

Make regeneration visible

Physical changes to estates are of symbolic as well as material importance. They have the capacity to communicate complex messages to a wide audience. Regeneration initiatives need to capitalise on this, perhaps by prioritising early action on strategic sites that are visible to outsiders. In addition banners and photographs could be placed in prominent places in order to reveal changes to the interior of the estates.

Draw non-residents onto the estates

Stigmatised estates are often physically isolated cul-de-sacs with few facilities to attract non-residents. Regeneration initiatives need to find ways to attract outsiders onto estates to use existing or new facilities there and to witness changes. Care will need to be taken to ensure that facilities designed to attract non-residents do not conflict with resident priorities.

Use local residents as advocates for their communities

Local people, properly resourced, supported and trained, can be effective ambassadors for the success of the regeneration effort. Their testimony is viewed as credible and authentic by non-residents, and their involvement in the communication process is also seen as evidence of a resilient community that is trying to help itself.

References

Ashworth, G.J. and Voogd, H. (1995) *Selling the city: Marketing approaches in public sector planning*, Chichester: John Wiley.

Cole, I., Kane, S. and Robinson, D. (1999) *Changing demand, changing neighbourhoods: The response of social landlords*, Sheffield: Centre for Regional, Economic and Social Research, Sheffield Hallam University.

MacFayden, L., Stead, M. and Hastings, G. (1999) 'Social marketing', in M.J. Baker (ed) *The marketing book*, 4th edn, Oxford: Butterworth Heinemann.

National Housing Federation North (2000) *Positive associations: Marketing, allocations and customer loyalty manual of current practices in the North*, Leeds: National Housing Federation North.

Power, A. and Mumford, K. (1999) *The slow death of great cities?: Urban abandonment or urban renaissance*, York: York Publishing Services.

SEU (Social Exclusion Unit) (2000) *National strategy for neighbourhood renewal: a framework for consultation*, London: The Stationery Office.

Taylor, M. (1999) *Top-down meets bottom-up: Neighbourhood management*, York: York Publishing Services.

Wood, M. and Vamplew, C. (1999) *Neighbourhood images in Teeside: Regeneration or decline?*, York: York Publishing Services.

Appendix A: Research methods

The case-study estates were selected so that all have:

- undergone substantial regeneration;
- a problematic image; and
- recognised the importance of addressing that image.

They were also chosen to represent different approaches to image management, and different housing market contexts. The research falls into three main parts: focus groups with residents and non-residents; interviews with key actors; and a mystery shopper survey of estate agents.

Focus groups

Focus groups were conducted in each area with residents and non-residents of the estate. Participants were aged 18-45 and in secure employment. Separate groups were held for renters and owners, and for people with different attitudes to the estate.

In total 209 individuals participated in the focus groups (see Table A.1). In Meadow Well no owners who wanted to leave the estate and fitted our criteria were found.

Interviews with key actors

Individual interviews were conducted with:

- key regeneration actors;
- local employers;
- representatives of local media.

The number interviewed in each area varied according to local circumstances, but included a minimum of four local employers and three media representatives. Interviews were designed to identify the nature of the image problem, and the ways different actors respond to that image and perceive their own roles in maintaining or challenging such images.

Mystery shopper survey

Researchers, posing as a potential home buyer, contacted estate agents selling low-cost property in each area. A total of 18 estate agents were contacted.

Table A.1: Number of participants in focus groups

| Tenure | Edinburgh | | North Shields | | Birmingham | |
	Pilton	Leith	Meadow Well	North Shields	Castle Vale	Erdington
Owners	21	17	10	18	20	17
Renters	18	16	19	17	18	18
Total	39	33	29	35	38	35

Appendix B: Summary of three estates

Meadow Well, North Shields

Built in the 1930s as part of a slum clearance programme, Meadow Well is approximately a mile from North Shields and a few miles from Newcastle. The housing is primarily semi-detached and built to high space standards.

The regeneration process on Meadow Well has been managed by the Meadow Well Single Regeneration Budget (SRB) Board since 1995, which is now coming to the end of its tenure. Total regeneration expenditure in the period is estimated at £15 million from SRB sources, and an additional £11.6 million through private leverage and £11 million of other public-sector funds.

There are approximately 3,000 residents, often with long-standing connection to the area. The estate has little ethnic diversity. Unemployment in Meadow Well is a long-standing problem, in February 2000 it was 15.1% compared to 6.7% in North Tyneside.

There are few estate based facilities apart from relatively new and high quality community centres and a housing office conceived as a one-stop shop for council services. In particular the estate has poor shopping. However Meadow Well is well connected by public transport to both North Shields and Newcastle, and is adjacent to the Royal Quays development which comprises industry, high quality leisure and shopping facilities, and expensive new-build flats and housing.

The estate has never lost the stigma associated with slum clearance, and in 1969 unsuccessfully attempted to address the image problem by renaming itself. However the former name – The Ridges – is still used locally. In 1991 the estate's poor local reputation was reinforced by confrontations between young people and police which received national media coverage. The estate continues to suffer media attention, and also is regularly investigated by university researchers, themselves contributing to an ongoing reputation as a problem estate.

The SRB has a wide range of strategic objectives including improvements to community safety, the environment, and housing quality and management. It is physical change to the estate which is most marked. Substantial areas have been rebuilt, the street layout has been remodelled, and both housing associations and private-sector developers have built new property.

The SRB have demolished around 750 homes, and new houses have been built both for sale and rent. At March 2000 there were 1,100 council properties, 370 housing association, and 170 owner-occupied houses, with a further 110 under construction.

Image management is not a strategic objective of the SRB Board and no specific resources are attached to the issue. However, changing the reputation of the estate is seen as a key priority. The main focus is on managing the media, with key actors choosing only to cooperate with journalists who are willing to focus on something positive.

Despite the low key and unresourced approach to image management, the estate can point to some successes. Local media are beginning to change their tone, with less use of phrases such as 'previously riot torn'. The regional newspaper and television station have both run positive series about the estate. Yet this has aroused some local resentment about the levels of investment which the estate is benefiting from, some feel to the detriment of other areas, and the estate continues to carry its poor reputation both locally and nationally.

Greater Pilton, Edinburgh

Greater Pilton comprises the estates of Pilton, Muirhouse, Granton, and Drylaw, and lies two to three miles north of Edinburgh City centre. Built between the 1920s and late 1960s, the area is flanked by areas of expensive private housing, by industrial sites and by a waterfront and beach area. The area has had a variety of house types including system-built deck-access blocks, pre- and postwar walk-up flats and traditional cottage and terraced housing.

Regeneration is led by the North Edinburgh Area Regeneration (NEAR) partnership, which was established in 1993 to oversee a comprehensive regeneration programme. Investment to March 2000 has been £76 million. Prior to this the estate has undergone various forms of housing redevelopment and tapped into a range of regeneration funding sources, most recently being designated a Social Inclusion Partnership area. There is strong community involvement in NEAR and in many aspects of the regeneration process. Additionally the Pilton Partnership, which has a community development and anti-poverty remit and works in the same area, helps to facilitate local consultation.

There are approximately 28,000 residents in the North Edinburgh area, with around 16,000 covered by the Social Inclusion Partnership remit. Around 3% of the population is from minority ethnic groups. There are strongly knit communities in the estate and high degrees of loyalty to their neighbourhood from many residents. Unemployment rates are historically higher than the Edinburgh average: in February 2000 unemployment across the city was calculated to be 4%, but it was 8% in Pilton and Granton wards, and 16% in Muirhouse.

The estate has flagship community facilities including a community arts centre, library and Millennium centre, and a number of leisure facilities. One of the two shopping centres is in the process of being remodelled, and there are ambitious plans for a 'Docklands' style development in the adjacent Waterfront area.

There are few employers based on the estate, but adjacent to the area are a number of manufacturing businesses, and there are other employment opportunities from nearby supermarkets, a further education college and hospital.

Built as a slum clearance estate Pilton has been stigmatised within Edinburgh for many years. Current problems with the area's image probably date to coverage of the city's drugs and AIDS problems in the 1980s. This led to the area being considered 'no-go' by some, and to local residents being denigrated by the press. The Irvine Welsh novel *Trainspotting* has cemented the estate's problematic image in the minds of the Edinburgh population at large and may have given it a nationally poor reputation.

NEAR has a wide range of strategic objectives and programmes on issues such as housing renewal, tenure diversification, raising local levels of economic activity, health, young people and so on. To date, most progress has been made on physical renewal with significant housing change. Progress on economic development and employment issues has been slower, and the social aspects of the programme are only now getting underway with health and community safety strategies about to be implemented.

Progress to March 1999 includes the demolition of around 1,300 homes, including the early demolition of a large and unpopular deck-access complex. A housing association and housing cooperative provide new housing for rent alongside Edinburgh City Council. New houses have been built for sale, and large numbers of flats have been renovated by private developers and sold on the private market. At 31 March 1999 there were 5,654 city council properties, 1,385 housing association and co-op properties, and 3,923 owner-occupied houses (including 2,769 ex-council right-to-buy properties) in the North Edinburgh area.

Alongside this physical, economic and social agenda, a Communications Strategy is in the process of being implemented by NEAR and its partners which addresses issues such as the profile of the regeneration programme, communications between partners, and improving the image of the area. A part-time dedicated PR officer is employed to coordinate this, and to increase positive media coverage and establish media liaison protocols.

The popularity of the new and low-priced owner-occupied houses and increased demand for tenancies on the estate – particularly for the housing association properties – provides some evidence that the image of the estate is beginning to recover. However, the estate continues to receive poor press coverage and, while the Edinburgh housing market is booming, prices in Pilton remain depressed and it is difficult for individual owners to sell their homes. The evidence of this research is that the estate's reputation continues to be problematic locally.

Castle Vale, Birmingham

Castle Vale is six miles to the north east of Birmingham and covers an area of 1.5 square miles. Prior to the regeneration initiative, much of the estate consisted of 1960s system-built housing in the control of the local authority, including a number of high rise blocks. However, there is also an established owner-occupied area.

The regeneration of the estate is being managed by the Castle Vale Housing Action Trust. Established in 1993 this well resourced government body will be dissolved in 2005. To March 2000 government funding of the HAT has been £96.7 million, and private funding and other leverage £48.2 million.

The estate is home to nearly 11,000 people in nearly 5,000 households. Its population is less ethnically diverse than in Birmingham as a whole (around 4% minority ethnic households compared to 26% across the city). While unemployment was recognised as a massive problem in the HAT's early years, unemployment is now substantially lower in Castle Vale than for the city as a whole (6.1% compared to 9.1%, February 2000).

The estate has a range of community and sports facilities, including swimming baths, stables, and a new football stadium. There are two shopping centres, one of which is being remodelled to house a new Sainsbury's superstore. It is close to a range of major employers at Castle Bromwich and adjacent to industrial estates.

The estate was built as a slum clearance scheme, and its image problem may have stemmed initially from this. In the late 1980s, it was considered a no-go area by some and there was lots of negative media attention particularly in relation to drugs and car crime. Residents and the HAT believe postcode discrimination took place, especially with regard to employment and credit.

The HAT's remit is to tackle both physical and social problems on the estate including housing, road design, crime and unemployment. Its aims include improving and redeveloping housing; improving quality of life through addressing economic, social, living, health and environmental conditions; providing an effective service as a landlord and working with the community to ensure that the positive changes are maintained after the HAT is dissolved.

Progress to March 2000 includes the demolition of around 1,500 homes, including 20 tower blocks, and the completion of 700 new build and 786 refurbished homes. Additional tenure diversification is being progressed through right-to-buy, the Tenants' Incentive Scheme and new build low-cost housing for sale. At March 2000 there were 1,587 HAT properties, 610 housing association properties, and 1,456 owner-occupied houses.

The estate's reputation is recognised as problematic by the regeneration initiative, but image management is not a separate strategic objective. Rather, it is said to run through everything the HAT does. The HAT's dedicated PR staff are mainly responsible for publicity materials about the regeneration process and the changes on the estate. Dissemination of this message includes a web page, an annual newsletter which promotes the regeneration process to outsiders, a more regular newsletter for residents and community radio. Other HAT staff take the lead on disseminating information about initiatives to residents and there are regular neighbourhood newsletters to tenants who are directly affected by regeneration work.

The HAT has monitored media coverage of the estate and the Trust since its inception, and is currently seeking more sensitive measures of both. It has recently turned its attention to media management, aiming at a more strategic approach that promotes the estate through residents and successor organisations. However, this approach is in its infancy.

There is some evidence that the image of the estate is beginning to improve, including Barratts' decision to build on the estate, Sainsbury's decision to locate there, and employers approaching the HAT seeking to employ residents. A royal visit last year was seen as another sign that things were changing. The HAT believe local media coverage has improved recently, although does still seem to highlight negative issues as well. The evidence of this research is that the estate does still have a reputation to overcome, although the highly visible demolition work and the siting of Sainsbury's have begun to alter perceptions.